The Three Keys to Self-Empowerment

Also by STUART WILDE

Books

THE TAOS QUINTET:
Affirmations, The Force, Miracles, The Quickening,
The Trick to Money Is Having Some!

and

God's Gladiators
Infinite Self: 33 Steps to Reclaiming Your Inner Power
"Life Was Never Meant to Be a Struggle"
The Little Money Bible
The Secrets of Life
Silent Power
Simply Wilde (with Leon Nacson)
Sixth Sense
Weight Loss for the Mind
Whispering Winds of Change

Audio Programs

The Art of Meditation
The Force (audio book)
Happiness Is Your Destiny
Intuition
The Little Money Bible (audio book)
Loving Relationships
Miracles (audio book)
Silent Power (audio book)

The Three Keys to Self-Empowerment

STUART WILDE

HAY HOUSE, INC.

Carlsbad, California

London • Sydney • Johannesburg

Vancouver • Hong Kong

Published and distributed in the United States by: Hay House, Inc., P.O. Box 5100, Carlsbad, CA 92018-5100 • *Phone:* (760) 431-7695 or (800) 654-5126 • *Fax:* (760) 431-6948 or (800) 650-5115 • www.hayhouse.com • *Published and distributed in Australia by:* Hay House Australia Pty. Ltd., 18/36 Ralph St., Alexandria NSW 2015 • *Phone:* 612-9669-4299 • *Fax:* 612-9669-4144 • www.hayhouse.com.au • *Published and distributed in the United Kingdom by:* Hay House UK, Ltd. • Unit 62, Canalot Studios • 222 Kensal Rd., London W10 5BN • *Phone:* 44-20-8962-1230 • *Fax:* 44-20-8962-1239 • www.hayhouse.co.uk • *Published and distributed in the Republic of South Africa by:* Hay House SA (Pty), Ltd., P.O. Box 990, Witkoppen 2068 • *Phone/Fax:* 2711-7012233 • orders@psdprom.co.za • *Distributed in Canada by:* Raincoast • 9050 Shaughnessy St., Vancouver, B.C. V6P 6E5 • *Phone:* (604) 323-7100 • *Fax:* (604) 323-2600

Editorial supervision: Jill Kramer   *Design:* Tricia Breidenthal

Miracles: Original copyright © 1983, 1988. ISBN: 1-56170-540-3

"Life Was Never Meant to Be a Struggle": Original copyright © 1987. ISBN: 1-56170-535-7

Silent Power: Original copyright © 1996. ISBN: 1-56170-536-5

Library of Congress Control Number: 2003113459

ISBN 1-4019-0350-9

07 06 05 04   4 3 2 1
1st printing, June 2004

Printed in Canada

I'd like to dedicate this
book to that part of us
all that yearns silently
TO BE FREE. If we honor it
and make it special, it will
carry us gently to a new land
and a new place . . . one where
abundance and SPIRITUAL
IDEALS resonate effortlessly
within us as a natural part of our
SOUL . . . that place where we are
truly empowered to BECOME MORE,
to become a different person.

Contents

Introduction

Within the three little books contained here lies the key to understanding that you're not alone. There's a mysterious power all around you. It's your life force—the *etheric web,* I call it. It's a force field that you emit from within. It's massively powerful, and it stretches out all around you. It's here to help you understand and grow. Through this invisible power, you're connected to all living things, so you can gradually pull to you whatever you need in this lifetime.

Self-empowerment is the act of raising your energy so that it resonates faster, and you become ever more powerful and capable with every day that passes. There's no limit to how far you can go, and eventually you'll find that whatever you concentrate on appears shortly thereafter in your life. That is the miracle of your silent power. It's tried and tested, and millions have come to understand their true power through this method.

I once met a South American lady who was working in New Jersey as a house cleaner. She followed the miracle-action plan, and two weeks later she won more than a million dollars in a lottery. I went to see her, and she proudly showed me a photo of herself at the presentation ceremony with the check. I can't promise you the same results, but even if you don't get a big payoff right away, there will certainly be many other blessings out there in the energy field waiting to find you.

I've used this power for 20 years, and I'd venture to say that I'm quite a good advertisement for it, because I've used it to help me make it in life. I found that the power granted me extrasensory perception, which I used to learn a lot about the subtle energies of life. I found that I could tap in to the etheric web through my feelings and not only see beautiful things beyond common knowledge, but also pull from it original ideas that I then put into my books to help others. You can do the same.

Something else you might try is meditating (if you don't already do so), for it is in the quiet time when your mind is silent that you see the full scope of the power that you are a part of. Your creative potential is in there, and there are many new ideas that will give you pleasure . . . or you might discover money-making schemes you hadn't thought of yet.

Once you see that you're not alone, you'll realize that you don't have to struggle as much as before. You can let go of many of the difficulties of life by replacing confusion with perception, and a heaviness of heart with a lightness of being. Our natural state is one of joy, and joy usually comes in the simplicity of things.

These keys to empowerment are simple to understand and easy to put into effect; it's very much a matter of changing your mind and opening up to allow the power of the life force within you to carry you along. It's all there waiting for you, and as you come to comprehend it better, people respond to your newfound energy. Suddenly, old blocks and frustrations fall away, and you find yourself better connected to the universal flow of things, your path becomes straighter, and people come forward to help you make new connections.

Overall, good things come to you as they should . . . *miraculously.*

✂⬤✂

— Stuart Wilde, 2004

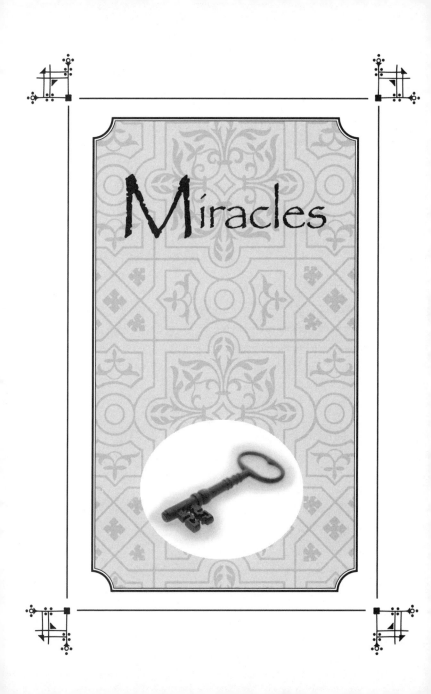

Miracles

Creating Miracles

Creating miracles in your life is no more complicated than understanding the metaphysics of the Universal Law. And because that law is indestructible and therefore infinite, we know that the power used by miracle-makers in the past is still available today. Yet, in our modern society, we're brought up to believe only in those things we can logically understand. We're not taught either that the Universal Law has limitless potential or that this power is at our disposal and can be used to work miracles in our own lives.

✺

Understanding
the Universal Law

To understand miracles, we have to look at two aspects of the Universal Law. First, there lies deep within all humankind an immense power; and second, the power is impartial and unemotional. Call it the Universal Mind, Christ Consciousness, or what you will, but it is this power that allows human beings a recognition of the universal life force that we call "God."

The life force is eternal and universal, and, because of its limitless capacity, it's a part of all things. Moreover, it's a major part of each of us. Consequently, we all have within us an *unlimited power*. Creating miracles in our lives becomes a matter of identifying with the power, understanding its characteristics, and learning to use it effectively. This identification is achieved by knowing that the power is within you and acknowledging that fact by saying, "I am eternal, immortal, universal, and infinite, and what I am is beautiful." In this manner, you lock into the power source and you're poised for the next step, which involves looking at its characteristics.

The Universal Law is impartial and unemotional. It has no way of knowing what you want, nor does it discriminate between your hopes and aspirations, likes and dislikes—it is pure energy. It accepts whatever thoughts, feelings, and actions you project and reflects them back to you unemotionally in the form of events that you experience day to day.

In much the same way that electricity illuminates both a brothel and the vicar's tea party, the Universal Law doesn't differentiate between different types of energy in your life. It will give you anything you believe in—no more and no less. Therefore, the key to understanding miracles is to look at the beliefs you express as thoughts and feelings.

When you're born, your thoughts and feelings are limitless because your mind is a clean slate. What a small child projects to the Universal Law is a natural purity unbounded by the constraints of beliefs. Children often attempt the seemingly impossible: Unaware that they have any physical limitations, they drive off in the family car or walk on a high ledge. It's only later, through education, that they learn the confines of human expectancy.

But these confines or boundaries are illusions. They are formed by belief patterns, most of them born of ignorance, handed down from generation to generation. This pool of belief patterns or "collective unconscious," as Carl Jung called it, gains validity as it moves through time, and eventually the concepts that later generations experience as physical reality become rigid and domineering. It's as if billions of people who preceded you have determined what you're going to experience on the earth plane, and that's all there is to it.

This rigidity doesn't allow for genius or for the understanding that we're now in an era of rapid unfoldment. Fundamental structures are being swept away in an avalanche of awareness, and we're no longer prepared to just read about great miracle-makers; we want to have the same experience. For most people, this isn't possible because they're locked within the limitations of body and mind; their upbringing is so dominant that it encases their entire evolution, and they experience little spiritual growth.

Understanding Life's Mission

[handwritten margin note: Course in Miracles - "I am not a body, I am free"]

We are not our bodies or our emotions or our minds or any of the structures and restrictions we experience around us. We are an infinite part of the God-Force, using the physical form to experience spiritual development through a special teaching called "daily life."

When you entered the earth plane, the energy that is the real you left its abode in the higher dimensions of pure light, and entered, by choice, the body you're now in. You chose the circumstances of this life because it was the next step in your infinite evolution, and because this life would allow you to expand what you are spiritually so that you could become an even greater expression of the infinite life force or Living Spirit.

Now, you may say: "That's nuts. Why would I choose these circumstances of my life—this family, this society, and this neighborhood? Why did I not choose a more affluent environment or a prettier body or more intellectual capacity?" The answer lies in a dimension beyond the physical plane. As you entered this dimension through birth, you had within your consciousness a heroic mission—a goal. The nature of that goal is firmly written in the very deepest recesses of the inner you, and what you are today, no matter what you feel about yourself, is actually a part of that goal in various stages of completion.

Your mind began recording events, thoughts, and feelings only at birth. It doesn't know of your heroic mission nor does it understand the Universal Law that interacts with your limitless potential. Why? Two reasons: First, if your mind, feelings, and emotions knew the nature of your heroic goal in life, there would be no challenge or quest, and your evolution would suffer. Second, most understanding of metaphysics is based on tribal or religious beliefs that do not totally reflect an accurate perception of the delicacy of energy and the way its ebb and flow affects daily life; no real understanding of the Universal Law has ever been incorporated into the various belief patterns of the world's collective unconscious.

For example, let's say that your heroic goal in life is to learn to love yourself and to accept full cosmic responsibility for what you are. And, let's say, you have had a number of previous experiences on the earth plane in which you were weak and indulged yourself metaphysically by leaning on others rather than contributing to your own energy or support. If you knew this in advance, you'd begin to favor one course of action over another. You'd intellectualize yourself into positions or feelings that you wanted to achieve, and your mind would dominate your every move. Evolution doesn't work that way. You can't overcome weakness by fighting it or thinking your way out of it. You overcome weakness by leaving it behind you. This means that you become aware of the inner tendencies that bring you down, that don't support a belief in self, that don't endorse a love of self, and you say, "I don't want to be that anymore." You then move yourself out of the slovenly ways of the collective unconscious, into a discipline of power. From time to time, you may drift back, but once you decide on the side of strength, the power of the Universal Law will always be with you to varying degrees.

It may be a battle at first, because your mind does not understand these laws or the nature of your mission on earth, nor does it understand the laws that govern your potential. It will have a tendency to "advise" you logically from its own experience, and logic is death to that part of you that is the miracle-maker.

><

Understanding the Nature of Beliefs

The next step in creating your own miracles is to look at the nature of beliefs. By reviewing beliefs and feelings, you begin to understand how to use the Universal Law effectively. It's natural to yearn for the impossible, and in so doing, you establish strong beliefs about what can be done and what cannot. You can jump a certain height and no higher, run at a certain speed and no faster, accept a certain position and no better.

Because most commercial aircraft fly at about 600 miles an hour, the shortest time in which you can get from New York to Paris is about six hours. Those are facts in the collective unconscious. But what if we told you of a man who could move his body many thousands of miles in just a few seconds? Your mind would scan its memory banks and draw a blank, whereupon you might think, *impossible*. Then perhaps you might review all the scientific data available and conclude that this feat is unachievable. All scientific knowledge and current thinking are products of the same collective unconscious, and just the fact that a billion people have no concept of a man moving 3,000 miles in a few seconds makes it impossible. But the billions of people are wrong.

There is a dimension, right here on the earth plane, in which such a feat is possible, and there are a few people alive today who know of this dimension and use it. It's a matter of perception and belief. Your ability to work miracles is predicated entirely on how easily and quickly you can give the collective unconscious the slip. It's your attachment to the collective unconscious, or world belief patterns, that holds you back.

This attachment, which you accepted at birth, is your main challenge in life, and your spiritual goal is to step above it. Eventually you realize that in order to become part of a higher consciousness, you have to leave where you are right now and step into the unknown. That's why all the tales of the path of the initiate talk about loneliness, for as you move away from old energy, there's a sense of loss.

As you take that step, your perceptions expand gradually to accept a higher vibration of self, and you understand that what others believe is a part of their evolution, but it's not the sum total of all the facts. We experience life through the five senses, "the windows of the soul," and we're taught what capacity those senses have. Yet, each of them has a dimension that's many times deeper than is normally perceived, and those dimensions will open for you as you move toward them.

Let us look at feelings. Through feelings, you can enter into other worlds, and clairsentience (a heightened sense of feelings) is a capacity you can learn to develop quite quickly. It's not as acute as extrasensory sight, but it's deep, and through it, you enter into areas of perception that few people ever experience.

Everything around you is energy—your body, its various organs, your thoughts, the physical place you inhabit, the events of your life—each expresses an energy. A part of that energy is perceivable through the five senses, but most of it is beyond normal perception. By opening to the power of the Universal Law and controlling the mind through centering and discipline, you become aware of the subtlety of energies around you. You'll find that you can use your feelings to guide you through life.

As you move into a situation, push your feeling into whatever lies ahead. How does it feel? What is the Universal Law saying to you? Which area flows, and which does not? After a while, this exercise becomes simple and very accurate. You may not be able to see all the subtle energies around you, but you can learn to feel them, and soon you'll find that information from the Universal Law has a way of jumping at you unexpectedly.

Events in your life gather energy as they come toward you, and you can feel that energy weeks and even years before they occur. Science will tell you that it's not possible to foresee the future, and that's true for those who believe it to be so, but as you move out of the world's "group perception," feeling and even seeing the future will become second nature to you.

To harness the Universal Law effectively, you should watch its manifestation, which is basically every event in your life. Then link each event to your underlying feelings and attitudes. Realize that when things go well, it's solely because you put that image into the Universal Law and it responded. Imagine the Universal Law as a shipping clerk in a large mail-order company. He gets your order but has no idea who you are. If the order says "size 8," he sends out size 8. It's of no concern to him whether or not size 8 fits you. He merely complies with your request.

In daily life, your feelings, thoughts, and attitudes are your order form, so before you decide to change your present conditions, you'll have to be very sure what you want from life. The Universal Law reacts spastically to uncertain messages. You have to write clearly, and you have to be ready to accept whatever you're looking for. Let's say you want to win a large sum of money, give up your job, and spend the rest of your days lying in the sun. You dream about the cash, and you sigh and say, "Wouldn't it be lovely." But is that actually what you want? You might very soon find yourself bored, and although your mind would like to lounge in the sun, the inner you might say, "I should have stayed where I was; there was more potential there."

Creating energy for yourself through the Universal Law isn't just a matter of wishing for things, willy-nilly. You have to realize that the power is within you, and once you take the first step toward it, whatever you create will be for your highest good. It might not be exactly what you thought you wanted, but you'd better be ready for the consequences.

Before embarking on a miracle "action plan," you ought to spend some time meditating on the conditions or material objects you want. The Universal Law is the shipping clerk waiting for your clear and concise order. The currency with which you're going to pay for it is *belief.*

To create something with absolute certainty, you have to establish the feeling within you that it has already happened—that the condition you desire is already a part of your life. This can be hard because your mind, knowing nothing about the workings of the Law, fights back.

You affirm, "I'm rich," and your mind contradicts, "You're not." The conflict that develops confuses the Universal Law, which is about to deliver your heart's desire. This clash of opposing energies has been the challenge of the would-be initiate since the beginning of time. It's the hunt for the Grail, or the slaying of the dragon. It states that no one enters the kingdom of heaven within until he has tamed the dragon of negativity that he inherited from the collective unconscious. Figuratively, you'll have to leave the earth plane even though you may still be very much a part of physical reality. Dimensions aren't out there someplace between you and the stars; they're inner worlds or inner journeys.

These journeys have an inner reality and an outer manifestation in the physical, so anything you can conceive is actually a part of you right now. The fact that you don't have it on hand matters not. Whatever it is that you conceive is in a state of gradually becoming. If you affirm, "I am rich," you have to start feeling rich, thinking rich, and holding a rich attitude. Walk around expensive stores, have coffee at the best hotel in town, and begin to act and feel as if you already have the vast fortune you know the Universal Law is about to deliver to you. In this way, you create a concrete reality of wealth within your inner journey, and it will become manifest in your outer journey, the physical world. If you can maintain that feeling and power and live as if your wish has already been granted by the Universal Law, your wish will be delivered, guaranteed.

100 % Commt

But you cannot be halfhearted, or you will dissipate your personal power and nothing will happen. You have to take to the path like a warrior. You're going to achieve your goal. No matter what confronts you, no matter where you are right now, no matter what adversity you face, you will reach your objective. The Universal Law does not care whether you have your heart's desire or not. Therefore, you might as well make up your mind to collect.

You can have anything you want, and when you create it, it becomes yours. Often we feel we don't deserve success or wealth or complete health or anything else we might yearn for. We're taught in childhood that we're not worthy, or that somehow we owe something to society or the physical plane, or that we have some kind of special sin that we should atone for before we can enjoy what we want out of life.

This is not the case. The Law does not discriminate. It receives your energy and delivers diamonds or plain rocks, depending on what you put in. It's very important to look at the negative feelings you have about yourself. It's easy to say, "Oh, I never win anything," or "I'm too old; they will never hire me," or "I can never be with that person; I'm not pretty enough." That kind of thinking is indicative of the mind and its "logical" advice.

Miracles are not logical, so the last thing you need is logical advice from the mind. When such advice is given, acknowledge the mind, thank it, and say, "I do not accept any energy that is contrary to the unlimited power that lies within me," then press on.

Infinite power is so magnanimous, so powerful, so much more than the mind, that it exists in a separate dimension, and that is why the mind has difficulty perceiving that it is even there. You will get an intuition or feeling or a rush of excitement, but that is all. You cannot really hear it, touch it, or taste it, but it comes 'round the mind like a breeze, and when it starts to work in your life, you will know it by the quality of the people and events that surround you.

Before we go to Step Four, the Miracle "Action Plan," let us briefly review some important points.

※ The Universal Law, or Living Spirit, is unlimited. This force is within you. Therefore, what you are is also unlimited.

※ The Universal Law is impartial and unemotional. It cannot discriminate. It will willingly give you anything you believe in.

❋ You are not your body or your emotions or your mind. You are a part of the Living Spirit, learning. No matter what your circumstances, the Universal Law can be called upon at any time because it is the *real* you.

❋ Whatever you create for yourself by understanding the mystical, metaphysical aspects of the Universal Law is yours—because you created it, you deserve it.

❋ Miracles are not gifts from God; they are a part of what you are, which is God.

Finally, the Universal Law is in balance and harmony by its very nature. And so, as you set out on your "action plan," you will not be able to infringe on others. Whatever you create will have to be for yourself. You cannot will the Universal Law on to others, saying, "I want this to happen to my friend." This would be infringing, because, not knowing the nature of your friend's heroic life plan, you're not entitled to change it or in any way alter what he's going through at this time. He has to experience life for himself, as he also has unlimited power within him, and a part of his growth pattern is discovering that fact.

Within the Universal Law, there's no dual energy, good and bad, saints and sinners. There's just energy—one power that pervades all things, and everything is a part of the power. Differentiation between good and evil is just your perception, for within real energy there is no judgment. There is high energy and not-so-high energy, and at the end of this life you will have the opportunity to review what you've achieved, which will be a matter of how much you've succeeded in centering your life in a discipline of perceiving the Living Spirit and using it. But your review will not be emotional. You will be looking at the quality (or speed, if you like) of the energy you created. If you've harmed others, you've impeded your evolution by decelerating the life force within you. That is your karmic energy, and someday you will have to understand that it was not your highest path. But you cannot judge others, because, since the energy your mind perceives doesn't incorporate the nature of their heroic goal, you have no way of knowing that what they are going through is not exactly what they need karmically for their growth at this infinite point in their evolution.

There are no accidents or victims. Each person is responsible for his own evolution. Each pulls to himself the circumstances experienced in life. He puts in an order, so to speak, and gets back three cracked cups. That is a part of the learning pattern, trial and error.

This lifetime is yours. You may be involved in relationships and love others, but basically what you make of your life and how you pass through it is your evolution. We all learn to take responsibility for our own circumstances, and, within the Universal Law, we're not expected to take responsibility for the evolution of others. It might sound a bit harsh, but in the Law there is incredible clarity and justice.

That is why adversity is so useful. It allows people to look for something beyond day-to-day reality, and this brings them in touch with their true inner selves. In desperation, they begin to pull on their *unlimited power*, and they realize that anything can be changed, that suffering is a product of the inner self, and by looking at their inner selves, they can transform them. It has been said that there are no incurable diseases, only incurable people, and this is true of all energy within the Universal Law. Trying to fix your circumstances just physically or mentally will not work in the long run because deep-rooted inconsistencies will continue to surface in your life in various guises. To overcome something once and for all means going within yourself to discover the real causes of the disturbance.

This process or discovery will allow you more energy, which you can use to create the things you want in your life.

><·><

The Miracle "Action Plan"

Write down on a piece of paper, in order of importance, the things and conditions you want. Don't
let the mind "advise" you; it has limitations. Shoot for
the moon, and be sure you leave nothing out. Chop
and change your list until you're comfortable with it,
but be clear about what you want. Use exact and precise wording to describe the conditions you require.
Remember, the system works, so you must be definite
in the way you describe your wants.

Here's what you do:

a) Read your list three times a day—once when
you rise, once in the middle of the day, and once
before bed.

b) Meditate on your miracles from time to time, and
KNOW that the Universal Law has received your
order and is just about to deliver.

c) Maintain silence. Talking about your miracles dissipates the energy drastically. Therefore, you cannot share your miracles with others until they happen.

d) Always act and think about your miracles as though you already have the conditions you desire.

e) Be open to the inner promptings of the unlimited power source as it instructs you in ways of getting what you want. Realize that the Universal Law has to deliver in the physical plane where you can make use of it. Your heart's desire can come from anywhere, so do not limit your field of expectation. Remain open and flexible at all times.

f) Smile a lot—the first miracle is on its way!

⌖

Understanding Energy

Since the mind has no way of knowing how the Universal Law is going to deliver your miracle, don't waste time trying to figure it out, just KNOW. Your thoughts should be like acorns that develop gradually into oaks; if you dig them up to discover how things are going, your tree will perish. It's important to avoid fretting. Center on the feeling that some way, somehow, the Universal Law will not let you down, because everything in the universe is energy.

Solid objects appear as such only because their atoms and molecules move at high speed. In fact, reality is both solid and not solid at the same time, and this applies to thought-forms. They're real, and even more powerful than physical reality because they're not constrained by the limits of the material plane. But you cannot take them apart and analyze them. You have to create them and let them fly.

Then through enthusiasm and belief, you energize the Universal Law and encourage it to deliver. Try at all times to keep your thoughts pure and on target. If doubt creeps in, don't allow it to dominate for long. Look at doubt from above yourself. Realize that it's just the mind fretting, not understanding, creating objections through ignorance, and whatever you have set in motion will happen.

As you work with the power, it will have a way of showing you the next move at every turn. Believe in it. Know that this inner force is so powerful that it will pull you into excitement and adventure beyond your dreams. Keep it pure, remain silent, and remember to keep your methods secret.

Everything that surrounds you has the Living Spirit within it in varying degrees. Living things express it more than do inanimate objects, but all have it. The more you come into contact with the Universal Law within you, the more you're in touch with things around you. Everything becomes a symbol and strength to you. The world helps you, and the fuller you become, the more dimensions you can pull from.

A very dear friend was walking along a street one day wondering what to do with her life. She was at a crossroads literally and figuratively. Life was flat. She craved inspiration and had asked the Universal Law to direct her. As she stepped from the curb, a passing car nearly knocked her over, and as it screeched round the corner, a book fell out of its trunk.

It was a book about man's quest for the Universal Power, and it changed her life. Shortly, she left that town and embarked on a whole new evolutionary path that, over a period of time, has taken her to great metaphysical heights and into countries and relationships she could not have conceived of before.

The Universal Law provided her with a special teaching in the form of that book, and she, being in tune, was ready to benefit. And so it should for you. As you work toward your miracle, watch for every sign, for every change around you, and you will see the Universal Law communicating with you. The more you trust it, the more the energy is encouraged to reveal itself, and various unusual things begin to occur. Your energy quickens, and opportunities pop up like corks on a lake. Then you will KNOW that the power is truly with you.

This coming in tune, more than anything else, will help you manifest your desires. You cannot act negatively in one part of the Universal Law and expect the other part to deliver your miracles unaffected. As you watch your life, you become expert at reading symbols, and you see that you are the only one responsible for what you are and that everything around you expresses an energy. The clothes you wear, the things you say, the people you associate with, the foods you eat, and the places you go are all statements to the Universal Law of what you are.

The quality of these statements, or the coming in tune with yourself and your surroundings, is the key to your spiritual unfoldment. What you are has great power. Its energy oscillates and reflects the amount of Living Spirit or God-Force that you express. The more you work on your life, the more you accept responsibility, the more energy you will have, and the greater will be your expectations.

Suppose you have a special project in mind and you want to be sure that you have the maximum possible energy available. Let's say you're heading for a job interview. You have put the job on your miracle list, the Universal Law has opened a door, and you're halfway there! Here's what you do:

1) Continue to see your miracle coming into physical reality. See yourself with the job granted until 72 hours before the interview, then forget about it.

2) On the day of your interview, rise early. Spend as much time as possible on your own. Avoid interpersonal conflicts. Tell the Universal Law that you're ready and willing to accept the miracle you've been asking for.

3) Abstain from such energy-lowering substances as alcohol and drugs.

4) Eat lightly. The Universal Law manifests *in* you and *through* you. If you eat great amounts of heavy food, your energy slows, and the Universal Law within you has difficulty expressing itself. You should have salads, fruit, natural healthy food, in sparing quantities. Stay away from junk food.

5) Before you set off for your interview, relax a moment. See the situation as flowing and positive. If you already know the person you will be meeting,

see him or her in your mind's eye, happy and smiling, receptive to your energy. See the interview going well; see the miracle delivered.

Understanding Time

Within the Universal Law, there is no time. Things are in a state of gradual evolvement. A tree has no concept of time because its essence is eternal. It responds to the warmth of the sun, but it is not "in time." It develops from seed, expanding gradually to full maturity, and so it is with the Universal Law. It can deliver instantly, but if your energy is not all there, it will seem to you as if it has taken time. You have to learn patience and keep moving toward your goal, knowing that your thought-form will be manifest.

If you're moving toward one particular miracle, and a different avenue opens unexpectedly, take it. The Universal Law delivers in strange ways, and what you think you desire may just be your way of expressing a totally different goal.

A good friend of mine wanted more than anything else to be a film director. He graduated from film school in London but found that he couldn't get any work because of a technical complication. To work in films in England at that time, you had to have a union card. But you couldn't get a union card unless you were working. In effect, the union created a "closed shop." My friend's miracle was stuck!

One day, out of the blue, he bumped into an old school friend who owned a restaurant, and due to his financial straits, he gladly accepted a job as a waiter. Working hard each day, he spent his spare time watching films and keeping his dream alive through study. Each day at noon, a well-dressed old man came into the restaurant. My friend served him diligently, and over the months the two of them became friends. One day my friend asked the old man what he did for a living. The old man replied that he was just about to retire from a job he had held for many years.

"What job is that?" asked my friend. "Oh! It's pretty boring, really," replied the old man, "I am president of the filmmaker union . . . not much ever happens."

Fifteen years later, I was flying across the United States, lazily watching an "in flight" movie when, to my great delight, I saw my friend's name on the credits of a major film. His miracle had been delivered.

When you move into an energy alignment, you can never tell what will happen. Watch for signs, use your feelings to help you decide, and if, after that, you're still not sure, do NOTHING.

If a direction is right, you'll know it automatically. If, however, making up your mind requires you to go through great trials and tribulations, you can be sure that that particular course isn't the one for you. Basically, it's good sense to remember that if you have to ponder a decision, it's usually a mistake. When the Universal Law delivers, you'll know it.

Start your miracle list with a couple of modest requests. Then, as you experience the Universal Law delivering, you'll feel the power of success around you, and that in itself becomes a valuable affirmation. Each time you reorganize your list, spend a few moments thinking about how well your last miracles worked. Affirm your power by visualizing your success; then, as you accomplish one miracle after another, you'll have the confidence to go to other things.

Understanding Your Personal Power

In conclusion, let's discuss how to establish an energy of power around you. Your mind's natural negative alignment will tend to make you think that your miracles are not going to come true. Therefore, in order to achieve complete success, you have to work constantly on your mind's doubt. Remind yourself that you're not your mind and you don't accept any energy contrary to your goals. In this way, you establish a pattern of positive affirmation in your life.

Write down in your own words nine affirmations that express your belief in yourself and your complete fulfillment in this lifetime. Three affirmations for the dawn, three for the day, and three for the night. Before reviewing your miracle list, relax, center your mind, then read your affirmations slowly. Make your affirmations strong, be sure that you feel their power and that they mean something special to you. The words and feelings that *you* believe in have the strongest energy. Here are a few examples from which you can build:

* I AM A POWERFUL, POSITIVE INDIVIDUAL, AND ALL EVENTS IN THIS DAY ARE FOR MY HIGHEST GOOD.

* WHAT I AM IS BEAUTIFUL, AND I PULL TO ME THIS DAY ONLY BEAUTY AND REFRESHMENT.

* THIS DAY IS A DAY OF BALANCE. I AM COMPLETELY AWARE OF MY BODY AND ALL ITS NEEDS.

* WHAT I AM IS ETERNAL, IMMORTAL, UNIVERSAL, AND INFINITE. I SEE ONLY BEAUTY AND STRENGTH EVERY MOMENT OF MY LIFE.

* I SEE ONLY BEAUTY IN ALL THE PEOPLE WHO ARE PULLED TO ME, AND WHAT I AM STRENGTHENS AND REFRESHES WHAT THEY ARE.

⁎ WHAT I AM IS INFINITE. I DO NOT JUDGE
   THE EVOLUTION OF OTHERS. WHAT THEY
   ARE RIGHT NOW IS FOR THEIR HIGHEST
   GOOD.

⁎ EACH ACTION I TAKE THIS DAY
   IS AN EXPRESSION OF THE GOD-FORCE.
   THEREFORE, EACH ACTION I TAKE IS A
   PART OF MY INFINITE CREATIVITY.

⁎ THERE IS NO REAL SIN, ONLY ENERGY. I
   FOLLOW THE ENERGY OF MY HIGHEST
   EVOLUTION AT ALL TIMES, AND SO BE IT.

⁎ I AM OPEN AT ALL TIMES TO COMMUNI-
   CATION FROM MY INNER SELF, AND THAT
   COMMUNICATION LEADS ME TO MY
   HIGHEST EVOLUTION.

⁎ I GIVE THANKS FOR THE BEAUTY OF THIS
   DAY, AND MAY THE ENERGY OF THIS
   NIGHT BRING RE-BUILDING AND RE-
   VIEW. SO BE IT.

Your affirmations act like small twigs in a fire. As you
arise, you begin to build energy in the day. Use your
affirmations to keep that energy going. Center for a
moment to acknowledge your infinite beauty and your
place in all things, then proceed.

If you're pulled into interpersonal conflict, take a few minutes on your own to repair your energy, and before going out into the day, be sure that your energy is strong. If you care for your power and you balance and center your life, no harm can befall you, and you enter into worlds that few people are even aware of.

Create your day the way you want it; see it going well; see each person you meet as positive and open to your energy; see the day as harmonious and flowing; and see yourself evolving through each and every experience.

Finally, before setting out into the day, see the white light of the Living Spirit around you, protecting you and strengthening what you are. Realize that the more you believe in yourself, the stronger the white light becomes. It acts as your shield, and from time to time each day you should reenergize it by seeing it vibrant and strong, and by affirming that what you are is a part of the Living Spirit, or God, and that each moment of your life is one of exhilaration and learning.

Your position on the earth plane as a miracle-maker is inherent in the infinite power that lies within you. That limitless source lies there waiting for you to step up and collect your heritage, and when you do, the power will always be with you . . .

. . . and that is guaranteed. So be it.

❦

"Life Was Never Meant to Be a Struggle"

CHAPTER ONE

The Strugglers' Hall of Fame

Do you remember being told as a child that if you wanted to make it in life you'd have to work hard? That life involves pain and struggle; that you'd have to earn love and acceptance; and that, if you wanted to come out on top, you'd have to put in an incredible effort? I certainly remember my mother saying to me, "Struggle ennobles the soul."

But who says this is true? Look at nature. It expends a certain effort in sustaining itself, but it does *not* struggle. Does the tiger in the forest get up in the morning and say, "I'll struggle like crazy today and hopefully by suppertime I'll get something to eat"? No way. It just rises, has a little sniff under its tiger armpits or does whatever tigers do at breakfast time, and heads out. At noon, there on the path is lunch, provided courtesy of the Great Spirit. Okay, the last 30 yards involves the tiger in a bit of rushing about. But that can hardly be construed as struggle.

You, too, may have to cross town to pick up a check. But there's a great difference between struggle and effort. Our physical condition as humans involves effort, but struggle is effort laced with emotion and desperation.

Think of this: If you accept full responsibility for your life, you'll accept that your destiny is created by you, and that your life is basically a symbol of your innermost thoughts and feelings—of what you believe about yourself.

Now if, over a period of years, you've laid down several hundred thousand thoughts in your subconscious that say, "Life is a struggle," naturally you'd project that from your inner feelings. Even if you weren't consciously aware of that aspect of your inner self, the thought would still lie deep within you and show up constantly in your life.

Whenever a project starts to flow too well, or things become too easy, your inner self emits an energy that says, "Warning! Warning! This is too simple. Let us self-destruct this project or relationship and come at it the hard way, so we can experience circumstances that are congruent with our inner belief that life is a struggle."

So things fall apart, and you feel like you're trying to push a peanut up Everest with your nose. Eventually, once you've suffered the slings and arrows of outrageous fortune for a while, the inner self pulls you to a watered-down version of circumstances that would have been yours anyway weeks ago and without effort.

This book helps you identify struggle, discover the reasons for it, and *eliminate* it. But first let us look at some of the characters in the Strugglers' Hall of Fame. I'm sure you'll have fun recognizing them from among your friends and acquaintances.

The Hero: Men like struggling, but then so do some women. The male version goes something like this: "If I bust a gut and run around trying hard, people will see me as a good man and treat me with respect. Whether I get results or not matters little, as long as I seem to be making a valiant effort. To make sure everyone acknowledges my heroism, I'll create an entire theater of frantic action, hectic schedules, meetings of earth-shattering importance, long hours, and constant pressure. Of course, this pantomime will make me a bit tense. But that's all part of the act, for the tension will be seen by others as my taking responsibility, and they will love and respect me for that. Won't they?"

If the truth be known, the answer is no. In fact, anyone with perception will see this male as a complete idiot. His weakness—namely a lack of personal acceptance, stands out a mile. He has chosen sacrifice as his fate in the hopes of winning affection or acknowledgment. His frantic actions only serve to underscore that he is out of control and hasn't a *clue* about what he is doing.

Another common struggler is **The Terrorist.** Because this fellow is uncomfortable with himself, he finds he can't deal with society. He was either born disadvantaged, has never been accepted, or he bears some other kind of grudge. He therefore has to operate outside of society and finds it hard to accept help from anyone. He struggles through a hundred and one projects that never quite come off. Even if he does make a success of a relationship or project, it seems to him a hollow victory—what he wants is acceptance, not success. So he'll usually self-destruct his successes, then move on to struggle at something else.

If the terrorist ever finds himself within the mainstream—if he gets a job in a corporation, for example—he'll find fault with that situation. He'll sneer at it and attempt to change or destroy it. Usually, his actions will threaten those around him—and sooner or later he'll be tossed out.

Because the terrorist has to *fight* the system rather than use it, he never gets what he wants. No one supports him. If he *does* find someone who loves and accepts him, he disregards that support, focusing instead on all those aspects of nonrecognition that are a part of his life.

The third type of struggler is the **Professional Wimp.** This person is so weak, so lacking in the ability to command life, that he allows everyone to lead him around by the nose. It makes him angry, and he will protest his rights from a position that he feels is logical and just. But his struggle results from weak energy. He gets nowhere and no one cares.

There is a variation on this theme: the **"Spiritual" Wimp.** This character has a huge ego and feels that God dropped him off on earth so he could sit around being "special." He is usually so "holy" that he can't soil his hands with life. He expects people to treat him like a god and to honor him anyway. Usually he struggles like crazy, for people find it hard to accept his lifestyle, and his failure threatens them.

One of the common female archetypes, **The Goddess,** is similar to the male. She plays a game called, "Please accept me, for I am great. I am really a goddess, and I am as strong as any male—or stronger." To act out her pantomime, she dresses in male clothes, drives fast cars, and gets superaggressive (to make up for her lack of confidence). And she, too, hurtles out and plays the achiever's game of her male counterpart.

In truth, being a goddess is hard work; you constantly have to sustain a celestial pose. Usually, others won't see you as a goddess, so you expend energy in the hope of convincing them. By trying to emulate the male, the female is actually saying, "I know I am weaker." This, of course, is not true. Most women are spiritually stronger than males, if only they would realize it.

Another female character has a play called **"Wilting Wallflower."** It goes like this: "I am just a helpless little person. I am weak and don't understand life. I can't add figures or mend a fuse; my emotions are all over the parking lot. Please save me, please look after me. That way I can sit someplace and not do much of anything."

This works to a certain extent, for sooner or later the "lifesaver" type shows up to assist her. The problem is that the lifesaver, be they male or another female, will only save the Wallflower once or twice. Then they move on because there's nothing in it for them.

As the Wilting Wallflower plays out her act, it gets harder and harder for her to feel any self-worth. Sooner or later that lack of self-worth pulls her to people who will delight in manipulating her. Her spiral of struggle is self-perpetuating for, in order to get the attention she craves, she has to create more and more dramatic scenarios of helplessness. Eventually she drifts into playing victim.

You all know the type. When you meet her, she pours out a litany of disasters. There is nothing you can do for her because she's not asking for help, she just wants you to commiserate. Quite often you will want to punch her in the nose just to keep her happy.

What do these characters have in common? First, they're all pretty stupid. They are playing out those facets of their personalities that are not truth. Yet, with just a small adjustment in attitude, they could move from struggle into flow.

You have to work hard at creating struggle, whereas flow is a natural condition. It comes from accepting yourself and watching your life so that it's reasonably balanced most of the time.

❧

CHAPTER TWO

Identifying Struggle

Because struggle is a programmed response and is natural to many, we often find ourselves struggling without realizing we're doing so. The first step in reducing struggle in your life is to identify it.

If you've read my book *Affirmations,* you may remember that I suggested that you take time to go into every aspect of your life, and evaluate what you get out of it in relation to what you put in. I asked you to plug in the "struggle-o-meter"—a mythical device created by your mind to gauge the levels of struggle you exert.

The main areas you review are as follows:

1) Your physical body
2) Your emotional balance

3) Your relationships

4) Your physical living circumstances

5) Your finances

6) Your attitude toward the world around you

7) Your ability to handle conflict

8) Your ability to handle stress

9) Your psychological state

10) Your spiritual balance

1. Your Physical Body

If your body is weak, it's either a genetic problem or an imbalance you created. If your weakness is genetic, you can change a "poor me" attitude to one of strength by realizing that your weakness is a gift. It allows you to express power in spite of your condition. It's like having one or two oarsmen in your boat and no oar for them. So what? The boat can make it anyway. A bit slower perhaps, but it will get there. And the extra time it takes will allow you to enjoy the journey more fully.

If your weakness is not genetic, fix it. Or at least express the most energy you can toward healing your body so that it doesn't dominate your life. As you put real effort into the healing, the rise in energy that results inspires you to go further. You will become happier and more balanced.

2. Your Emotional Balance

Emotional turmoil is yet another programmed response. As children, we're taught to cry out to get what we want—and sometimes we carry that over into adult life. "If I create enough fuss, will you love me?"

Your reaction to an emotional situation is just your opinion; it's not necessarily truth. In any given situation, you can react dispassionately or otherwise, as you wish. Train yourself to be more forgiving of yourself, more detached, and you'll see your life in an infinite sense—not a finite sense. Everything becomes a lesson, a way of strengthening you.

Gauge the level of your emotional rage. Everyone has it. If it comes up within you, do something positive to release it at once. Communication usually works.

Also, avoid conflict. Remember—only the fool stands and fights; the sage walks away. It's pointless to get your knickers in a twist if a certain person fails to react the way you want. It's best to avoid people and situations that drive you crazy. Remember to vote with your feet. If a situation is untenable or unchangeable, walk away.

3. Your Relationships

Through relationships we learn about ourselves, because people around us reflect back to us what we are. That is why many relationships are hard. If your relationships cause you to struggle, ask yourself why. What opinion do you hold about the relationship or yourself that prevents it from going the way you want? What are you trying to push against? What is your level of giving and receiving? Are you allowing yourself to be ripped off, and, if you are, is that okay, or do you want to change that?

4. Your Living Circumstances

Are your circumstances designed to nurture you? Do they support you? Or are you at the mercy of circumstances? If so, what are you going to do about it? What is the level of struggle here? For example, does the home you live in take so much effort to maintain that you get out of it less than you put in?

5. *Your Finances*

The question here is not, "Do you have enough money?" Rather, it is, "Is your life contained and balanced within the money you *do* have?" If it's not, you'll usually find yourself struggling to maintain a lifestyle that your ego/personality feels it needs, but which your current energy may not be able to sustain.

6. *Your Attitude Toward the World Around You*

Your life—your evolution—is your business; what others do is their business. If you let the world affect how you feel, what you're saying is, "I do not make my own decisions, I just have a Pavlovian response to anything that may twang my emotions."

Are you struggling to fix the world? If so, why? It's a bit of an ego trip when people think they can fix things. If you can see the world as an infinite evolution—the way God would see it—you would know that it's more or less perfect and does not need fixing. It's only when we view the world within the finite context of our emotions and ego that it looks less than perfect.

You can instantly become happy and free by deciding to leave the world alone and concentrate instead on yourself. By strengthening yourself, you serve all humanity. Each of us is linked to one another.

7. *Your Ability to Handle Conflict*

Conflict is always just a divergence of opinions. Are you struggling to convince others that your opinion is right? And if you are right, so what? To win a moral victory at the expense of your sanity is dumb.

8. *Your Ability to Handle Stress*

In a crowded world, with all the obligations we take on, stress is natural. Do you react emotionally or unemotionally to stress? Do you understand how to handle it? Some top-notch strugglers like to create stress so they can feel excitement in their lives. They live on their adrenals. You don't have to go bananas in order to have fun or to feel exhilarated about life.

9. *Your Psychological State*

If your psychological state causes you anguish, it will be either a by-product of your physical state or, once more, of your opinion. How much of each applies to you?

10. *Your Spiritual Balance*

Balance is natural. Whenever you force something to happen, you have to come off-balance to do so. How much do you exist in the flow? And how much do you have to push?

The difference between a spiritual person and a person who is less evolved is that spiritual persons are *real*. They live within the truth of the inner self, what many call the Higher Self. They don't play games; they don't have to make excuses. They can say with conviction, "I am what I am." They realize that they are neither all-knowing nor perfect and are happy with that.

Because people are generally weak, they tend to be phony and play out a character who is not them—who is not truth. So they struggle to maintain a Jekyll and Hyde existence. One is the official image the ego/personality says has to be maintained, and the other, what they really are. Often, people are so settled in their ego's reality that they won't realize what the Higher Self within is telling them. They see the fake character as real and will struggle to maintain that. Their energies and lifestyle become so fragmented that every effort to achieve anything becomes a painful grind.

⤛◈⤜

CHAPTER THREE

The Strugglers' Hit Parade

On the following pages, I've listed 11 of the most common reasons or aspects of struggle—the Strugglers' Hit Parade. Do any of these apply to you? If so, let's look at that. In the next section, I'll give you a powerful action plan to go beyond this.

1. Strugglers Crave Acceptance

Most strugglers have low self-esteem. This causes them to constantly seek the acceptance and approval of others. Yet the acknowledgment they seek is rarely forthcoming, and usually doesn't satisfy them even when they get it. This causes frustration. Because they lack a sense of identity, a sense of knowing or accepting who they really are, they shift their attention from what is real—inside themselves—to the symbols of life, which aren't real—outside themselves. They see the *things* around them as confirmation that they're okay, rather than confirming who they're within themselves.

Thus, life for them is a struggle to sustain a status that's fake. And no amount of baubles or bangles will keep this struggler happy, for acquisitions have only short emotional shelf lives. If strugglers buy, say, a new yacht, they can say, "Please accept me because I own this yacht." They're excited for a while as they play out the theater of yachting. But sooner or later, the emotional pleasure of the yacht drains away, and they then have to go and find something else to fill their acceptance needs.

If, by chance, life doesn't go the way the struggler wants, they get mad and frustrated—because now they are detached from their confirming symbols. They not only feel worthless, but they don't have the confirmation they constantly crave.

2. Strugglers Often Have Big Egos

Strugglers usually have big egos because they allow their egos/personalities to talk them into a greater opinion of themselves than they can sustain. It has to be exaggerated because they don't believe, or see, worth in what they are. So naturally, to compensate, they exaggerate life in the hope that at least some of it will come off.

You are divine spirit within a body, and you are finite ego/personality. The divine spirit or Higher Self knows the direction in which it is headed and has most of the power—the inner power. The ego holds the outer power. When your ego/personality is going in the same direction as the Higher Self, things flow. But if the ego/personality is off in another direction, struggle ensues. Remember, spirituality is being real, living in truth. The ego/personality lives in a variation of the truth, which is its opinion.

3. Strugglers Feel That Struggle Is Noble

To justify the fact that their lives are out of control, strugglers like to feel that struggle is noble—that somehow God is pleased with them for struggling. If you were God, you would fall over laughing at that one.

4. Strugglers Set Unrealistic Goals

The ego/personality decides what it needs to keep itself happy, and it decides how fast it wants those circumstances to come about. Often the struggler will set goals that are unrealistic. They may decide on a level, and say to themselves, "I will have that in six months." But their energy is not there yet on a metaphysical level. So there's a variance between what they *believe* is possible and what is *actually* possible. Usually the struggler will be impatient and push like crazy to make the deadlines they've set.

In that headlong plunge for the goal, strugglers gather a metaphysical wake around themselves, similar to the wake of a ship. That wake is hard to operate with, for their lives will lack fluidity. The wake creates an energy that is impossible for the Higher Self to penetrate.

They will be heading north, say, and the Higher Self will be whispering, "South, south," but the struggler does not hear it. The struggler sees only the goal, not the path. They're trapped by their opinion of how to reach the goal. No other possibilities exist. So life moves out of their way, leaving them to operate in a barren land. The strugglers are forced to head in the direction they've set for themselves.

Often, in the frantic effort to make the goal, they miss the side-turning that would offer simplicity or a shortcut. This kind ploughs on regardless of pain and anguish, or of whether their actions are appropriate or effective.

5. Strugglers Lack Understanding

Strugglers lack understanding. Sometimes it's just a lack of knowing about the physical plane and how the marketplace works. Usually the strugglers will have dropped out sometime back and be drifting, for they are not really prepared to concentrate on life and learn how the world works. They usually can't be bothered—struggle is easier.

It's common for this type to feel that the world owes them a living, and they get upset when circumstances do not agree with that point of view.

They also lack metaphysical knowledge. They don't see how the Universal Laws operate in their lives. So, rather than create an energy and let life come to them, gradually and in its own time, they go after life—and push it away through their needs and emotion.

6. *Strugglers Worry What Others Think*

Strugglers are often very social animals. They believe in a social reality, and they accept the opinions of others as truth. This forces them to live up to what are often the unreal expectations of others. They worry about what others think of them because they are not sure of themselves.

To go past this trap, all you have to do is to realize that your evolution through life is sacrosanct. You're the only one who can decide what's best for you. Only you have the answers. What society thinks of you is totally irrelevant, for others do not have all the facts. Remember, people will always try to manipulate you into their way of thinking. They will want you to act in a way that supports them. When you no longer feel the need to win their approval—because basically you have won your own approval—their manipulations of you become meaningless.

As with little children, you can love them for the games they play, but you do not have to take part. You can walk away. In the end, the only true path for you is as an independent. It's only a matter of habit and the way you learn to react. By detaching you become free.

7. Strugglers Lack Stability

Stability is the key to a worry-free existence. This means balance in every area of your life. This topic is dealt with extensively in my book *The Force,* but let's encapsulate the main point, which is:

To have balance and stability, you have to exercise control over every area of your life. This may not be possible as yet, but you can move toward total self-realization bit by bit. This means you're not going to let life tow you around. You'll develop the power to say no to situations that are not a part of your overall intention for yourself. You are the general of your army, making choices that constantly move you forward, toward that higher energy you seek.

It also means that you have the right to be satisfied with what you have and with what you are right now. Otherwise, you'll never reach a point where you're satisfied. You have to be happy with your lot right now. Just because your ego/personality may have sold you on an alternative program, it doesn't mean that you can't settle within the one you have now. There must be lessons to learn here and now. If those lessons aren't learned, if you don't accept what you've created for yourself, your energy does not move forward. By resisting, by not adapting to change, you stagnate. Some professional strugglers love to bang their heads against the wall—it feels so good when they stop.

Today is part of your life's curriculum. Learn it and tomorrow will look after itself. Think of this: If you've made it through life so far with what you know, it's obvious that you will make it through the rest of your life once you possess greater knowledge and objectivity. That is truth.

8. Strugglers Often Lack Concentration

Concentration is a key discipline in personal growth and development. Everything else is meaningless, for your power rests where your consciousness flows. When you're centered and concentrating on what you're doing, you not only derive more from your actions, but all your power—inner and outer—is being used to empower your actions.

The mind hates to concentrate. Most people cannot center on one idea for more than a minute. Now if you train the laser light of your intention in a direction, you empower that direction with your energy. If 15 seconds later you are distracted by a thought—"Did I leave the iron on?"—your power has gone.

By developing a goal, concentrating on it for a few seconds, and then becoming distracted—*and* by concentrating at various levels of intensity—you put into Universal Law such a hesitant, staccato message that it doesn't know what the hell you want.

Successful people set up a plan of action and concentrate on it until it's completed. Then they set up another. While working on an idea, they give it their full attention, empowering it with their consciousness until it becomes a reality.

Watch how your mind plays games with you. Often we start a project, and 15 minutes later the mind goes, "I hate having to concentrate on this. Let's have a cup of coffee." And so the project is put to one side. Or perhaps the phone rings; the caller has no idea what you're doing; their intention is expressed out of their need to speak to you. We allow the mind to use the telephone call to distract us rather than saying to the caller, "Thanks for calling, but I can't talk to you now; call back at Christmas." Through concentration you become powerful. Force your mind in order to concentrate, and you've won a battle over struggle.

9. *Strugglers Have Poorly Designed Lifestyles*

You are the general. Plot your battle plan and stay centered on it, but let the winds and currents of life allow you to flow to other areas. Designing your life is a matter of discipline. You need certain things, and you deserve them. But how do you get them with minimal effort? By cutting out those things that are superfluous. Toss the extra baggage out, and hold on to a life of simplicity. Constantly evaluate circumstances to see if things are worth the effort. Often you'll find that they're not.

10. Strugglers Lack Order

To go beyond struggle, you have to have order. Otherwise you dissipate energy, wasting time in confusion.

11. Strugglers Lack Concerted Action in the Marketplace

You're a consciousness, a spirit, but you're also a physical being. There's a point when you'll have to take your creativity to the people and sell it. That involves concerted action in the marketplace. Strugglers don't like concerted action. Yet through it, you get what you want.

✕

CHAPTER FOUR

Dumping
Struggle

There's no greater gift to yourself and to those around you than your deciding to dump struggle, for struggle is an unholy battle that you fight with yourself. It's not natural. Here are eight pointers you may wish to consider as you move from toil and struggle into absolute freedom.

1. Opinion

That which is struggle to one person is just gentle effort to another. Struggle is always how you feel about something—your opinion. It's laced with negative emotion. To dump struggle, you should get used to asking yourself in each circumstance, "What is my underlying emotion or opinion here?"

Perhaps your circumstances aren't really a struggle, and all you have to do is make a few slight changes in the way you view things. Usually the correction can be made simply and easily.

2. Timing

If things don't flow, ask yourself, "Am I going too fast? Or am I too slow? Is this the right time?" A great idea may result in a total flop if presented at the wrong time. Usually, things take longer than we expect them to. This is because we can think faster than we can act. So ideas need time to incubate and come together, especially when you need others to help you materialize your dreams. They must have time to become comfortable with your idea and to make it their own, to move through whatever considerations or opinions they may have.

Sometimes you may be moving too slowly. This may be through a lack of resolve or laziness or just plain dithering. To make life work, you have to face it full-frontal—head out with a good plan and trust in the Great Spirit to deliver. But head out toward your goal even if it seems a long way off. Nothing will carry you. You'll usually have to carry yourself.

Moving gracefully toward your goal, you enjoy the journey and watch constantly to see if your actions are in keeping with whatever energy you need to consummate your desire.

3. Cast of Characters

At this time, the world has more than five billion inhabitants. They are the characters you will invite to be in your army of helpers. Most will not be suitable, and many others will be busy in campaigns of their own.

But some are eminently suitable. To go beyond struggle, first you have to be able to accept the help of others, and, second, you have to choose your characters carefully. If you find yourself in a campaign with the cast already set, you must become a crafty general. You must get the most out of your people—given the circumstances, the goals, and what the budget allows. It's a mathematical certainty that you'll eventually eliminate most of the people who come into your life. We tend to think that the characters we have around us are the *only* characters. Not so.

I used to think that if I didn't get along with the kids in the neighborhood, I would have no friends. So I adapted to what I felt they wanted of me. Truth is that there are billions of kids all over the place—but coming from my finite view as a small boy, I didn't see that.

Never be afraid to let people go if they're not right; often that's the only way you can make room for the right person. Also, you're doing them a service. If they're square pegs in round holes, they need your help to move on to a more comfortable setting.

4. Is the Army Marching Without Boots?

To successfully materialize a battle plan, you have to go into the nitty-gritty. Do you have the wherewithal, the components you need? Or are you signing yourself up for a glorious disaster? Remember, just because you have a good idea, that's absolutely no reason to embark on it. Just because you love someone is no reason to marry them.

Let's say you want to open a store. Do you have the capital? What do you know about shopkeeping? Is there a market for the products you want to sell? It's amazing how many people open businesses without ever finding out if there's really any demand for that business. They feel that because they really like pink shirts with little dots, everyone else in town will. Not so.

A good general does not commit his troops until he knows what he's getting into. For example, if you want to start a magazine in the USA, it takes about a half-million dollars and five years to make it a financial success. Most new publications fold because the creators just don't know that simple fact.

Ask yourself prior to committing to anything, "Do I have the wherewithal to pull it off, and do I know what I'm getting into?"

5. Am I Trying to Capture a Castle I Don't Really Need or Want?

What is your motivation for taking action? What is the level of your commitment? And do you actually want the end result, or are you going for something else

example, are you dating the brother so
near the man you actually love? Is it worth
the effort—or is there a simpler way?

In *Warriors in the Mist,* the five-day intensive seminar I
used to put on in Taos, New Mexico, there's a section called
"The Quickening." You learn to speed up your etheric
energy and to evaluate your every move. You do this in light
of the speed at which things materialize in your life.

Expending energy in a wasteful way is the road to
poverty and struggle. You get bogged down in your own
inefficiency. Eventually your life becomes an affirmation of helplessness. Remember, most of the paths you
will be offered are totally inappropriate for you. At
every turn, give yourself five good reasons for saying no.
And while walking into a relationship or project, look
for the exit!

6. Am I Resisting?

To go beyond struggle, you have to go beyond rigid
opinion. That means opening yourself up to change.
Look to see how many paths there are available to you that

you can easily identify. And look at how many possibilities you may have missed.

A young businesswoman came to see me recently. Over lunch she explained a business deal she was considering. Maneuvering the salt and pepper shakers across the table, she showed me how the deal would net her $100,000. She wanted to know what I felt about the plan.

As we talked, the waiter brought a finger bowl to our table and placed it haphazardly between the salt and pepper shakers. Suddenly, I saw that if the deal were divided into two parts it would change dramatically.

I asked if this was a possibility.

"Yes," she replied.

In analyzing the situation, we discovered that, expressed in its divided form, the deal would net her $480,000. She went away with her battle plan. The event reminded me that there's always more than one way to skin a rabbit.

Look at your options. Then play the devil's advocate and look for all the angles you may have missed.

If you find yourself in an uphill situation, ask yourself, "What am I resisting? What is it in this situation that I have missed and that is causing me turmoil?"

7. Am I Content with Conditions?

It always amazes me that people will put up with difficult conditions and actually like them. If conditions don't suit you, then set about changing them.

8. Am I in Control?

What is the level of control you exert? Are you rushing around like crazy? Have you relinquished control to others? If so, why? Was it because you felt powerless? Perhaps it felt comfortable to allow someone else to drive the bus? Why?

By exercising control, you command and become responsible. You also have the ability to alter things to suit yourself. And you're not prone to the whims of others.

Remember, it's okay to get what you want from life.

⨯⬤⨯

CHAPTER FIVE

Conclusion

The very nature of our existence on the earth plane involves us in a certain amount of restriction. That is one of the lessons you come here to learn. Once that lesson is learned, you can move from restriction into absolute freedom, because ultimately your spiritual heritage is to be independent and free.

Effort is a part of our condition as physical beings, for we have to translate thoughts and feelings into physical action.

Struggle, however, is not natural. It's an unholy battle we fight with ourselves. But because it's a by-product of our personal imbalances, it's a condition we can easily go beyond.

By having the courage to identify and face the causes of struggle in your life, you grant yourself the power to transcend. Once you accept that *you* are the cause of struggle, you can then affirm, with certainty, that all struggle in your life can be eliminated, given time.

Further, because struggle is a programmed response—meaning that everyone is taught to struggle from an early age—it may take time to reprogram your attitudes for a more carefree existence. But it's fun to see yourself move gradually from various forms of anguish into celestial acceptance of yourself and the world around you.

To be free is a great gift. To achieve that, you do not need great amounts of money or influence or power. All you need is the ability to place yourself in a nonconfrontational mode. First, with yourself, and second, with the world around you.

As struggle begins to melt in the light of your balance and positivity, the new energy brings a freshness to your life, allowing your emotions to take on a resonating inner calm.

Inner calm allows you to pull more and more opportunities to yourself, because energy seeks its own kind. Balance and great good fortune can only come to a person who is balanced and feels fortunate.

Each day, from this moment on, toss out one aspect of your life that causes you difficulty. Make a note of your progress. See yourself moving inexorably toward your final goal—total freedom, exquisite happiness, absolute calm.

Once you reach that point and are able to sustain it for a while, teach it to others. Teach them that life was never meant to be a struggle.

They will thank you, for you will have set them free.

Silent Power

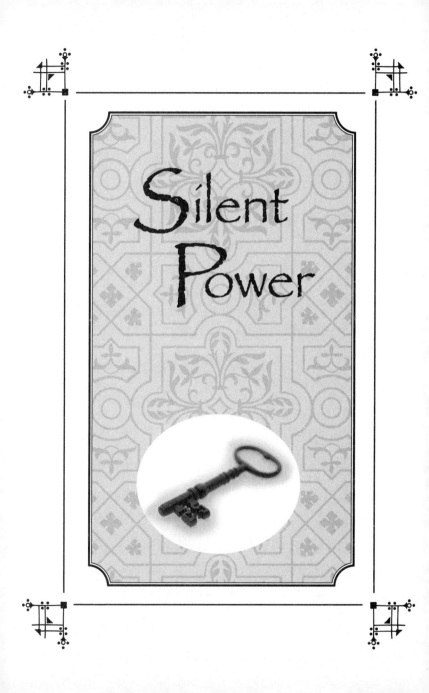

CHAPTER ONE

The Getting of Wisdom

Every so often you meet a person who's very different. You can't put your finger on what it is that attracts you to this individual, but he or she exudes a mystery and strength, radiating a silent power that's strange and beguiling.

What is this unseen force? Why do some have it and most do not? Here within these pages, I'll tell you about the power, its mystery, and how to get it. There's a simple trick you have to learn. Once you have that, silent power becomes your unspoken credential. It's a charisma that gradually grows and develops around you. Through it you can express a special goodness that helps people— and this planet—to change for the better.

From your silent power comes flow; from that flow comes simplicity of heart; from simplicity of heart comes contentment.

Some people, such as martial arts masters, gain silent power over the years anyway. They do it via emotional control and physical discipline, which quiets their energy naturally. They exude an effortless strength. Physical exercise and discipline are valuable in developing silent power, because they help you control the destructive side of the ego. But you need more than just a good physique and fitness—you need awareness as well.

Now, a little hocus-pocus. It doesn't matter if you don't believe in hocus-pocus; the basis of this concept is real enough. You don't have to worry too much about technical details. Put the intellect aside, and cut to a technology that works. That's my way.

Around you is an electromagnetic body of energy that is sometimes called the subtle body and is normally unseen by the naked eye. The ancient Greeks called it the etheric body. This is where the *real* you resides. It's also where your real feelings reside.

Imagine it to be a faint energy field, like a colorless mist. But, unlike a slow, wafting mist, the etheric is moving very, very quickly. Flashing through it are mini-lightning bolts of energy, and fingers of flame-like etheric sunbursts that shoot out from you in all directions. Underlying the flashes are great waves of rolling energy that move up and down and sometimes outwards, tumbling and turning in response to emotion. You walk inside an amazing glowing bubble of light that sometimes projects three to four feet away from you in every direction.

The etheric is fascinating and beautiful to watch. I find it very humbling—the *secret* human is all there to see, spiritually naked in his or her identity. In that vulnerability dwells the very essence of our human experience—painted in the electromagnetic flashes, wisps, and lightning bolts that are projected from you.

In the etheric, you see how the human condition is complicated by the ego/personality, but you can have a deep compassion for it. For a human is not just a mind, a body, or an emotion—it is light. The brilliance of that human light overshadows the personality traits and weaknesses that come from human frailty.

In the vitality of the light is the sacrosanct identity of the eternal spiritual being. The presence of this wonderful gift of the etheric body grants you a silent power as ancient as time. It is the spiritual heritage that flows from your connection to the God-Force.

With a little training, you can sit and watch the fascinating etheric dance to which we all belong. I surmise that many of the great unexplained metaphysical mysteries are contained within it. Later in this book, there are several exercises to increase your etheric perception. But seeing the etheric is not as important as knowing it's there, projecting it correctly, and learning to perceive it via your subtle feelings.

After 12 years of experimenting, of watching people, I can guarantee that the light is definitely there. In fact, I have never seen an animal or a human who didn't have an etheric. On an energy level, it's the blueprint of the real human. Coming to see what works etherically and what doesn't has been a slow process for me, but it has been worth the effort, for the mysterious world of the etheric is one of the last unconquered frontiers. It's where everything is explained: hands-on healing, subliminal energy, charisma, power, telepathy, extrasensory perception, and perhaps even the mystery of life and death itself.

I'm now convinced that, on a subtle level, everyone is subliminally aware of the etheric. When you reach out with your mind and touch other people's energy, they feel it. Often they turn around, blink, or respond in some way. They react, even though they don't know why. When two people meet, you can watch an etheric process take place. A synapse fires across the empty space between the individuals; the energy of each mingles momentarily with the other, exchanging trillions of pieces of information in a split second.

We have each had the experience of others reacting to us; often there seems to be no logic to it. But, in fact, people do pick up on our subtle energy, and even if they can't see it or put it into words, they feel it and, subliminally, they know. They vote yes, no, or maybe, according to the qualities and strength of the energy we project.

The power of your etheric is made up of several factors: the speed at which it oscillates, the intensity of the energy (how much is happening at any one moment), and the consolidated or contained nature of the field. In an untrained person, his or her etheric is flashing its wispy fingers of energy out all over the place—touching others, interfering with them, often sucking energy from others, impinging on them. The vish, the intensity is weak; sometimes it is torn, usually through an excess of drugs and alcohol, and has no solid definition. It reacts a lot to emotion, wobbling and slopping about like an enormous pile of jelly on a plate—rocking, rolling in jerking spastic motions, back and forth.

Of course, you don't have to see the etheric in order to work on it, repair it if it's damaged, and make it strong. Because it expresses what you are, it's affected by your whole state of being, including your physical condition, your mental and emotional balance, and your fortitude. All this manifests as a sense of well-being—how alive you feel, how secure you feel, and how you view the eternal spiritual self that dwells within.

So the first step to the mystery of silent power is to strengthen your psychological and emotional attitudes. This will boost your sense of well-being. It will also help you externally, as people will see from your body language, by what you say, and by your general attitude, that you are strong. Intellectually, they will *think* you're strong, but inwardly—at the subconscious level—they will feel and *know* that you are strong. They will automatically react positively.

People like controlled strength; it makes them feel safe and supported.

Come—let's start by considering what power really is, and then we'll discuss leaning and not leaning. I'll show you something obvious, something that 99 percent of the population don't see.

><

CHAPTER TWO

The Power Hungry—
The Power Starved

◆

What is normally considered to be power is not real power at all. Chasing money, glamour, sex; wanting control over others—political and military power—are all manifestations of the ego. They are often glorified forms of showing off; they dwell in the currency of the ego, and they often appeal only to other egos, so they are subject to people's whims. A person can be rich and successful and still be very weak. Money doesn't give you real strength; it just keeps you comfortable while you experience your dysfunction. The world of the ego is brittle, fragile, and insecure; it never feels really safe, and it has no lasting worth. The ego's world dies. More often than not, it self-destructs.

With the explosion of the mass media and the information superhighway, glamour, hype, and showing off have replaced true worth. The 32-second sound bite is more important than real facts. A glossy, skimmed-down version of life is all anyone has time for, as each vies with the other for a momentary place in the sun.

Many people are victimized by their egos; they feel power-starved, so they crave to be special. Of course, everyone is special in their own spiritual way, but the mass media has heightened people's need to seek fame and attention. Thirsting for power, in the ego's sense of power, they go through the ludicrous chase of trying to be important, trying to become special in the eyes of others, seeking praise, seeking status. This frenetic chase destroys and saps their energy.

Because the ego is insecure, its fears need to be quelled, so it dominates our psychology, firing off endless demands. It desperately wants things—right now—that will help it feel better. We are programmed as children to make the ego important and to try to keep it happy, and this mesmerizes us into reacting to its every need.

We don't realize that controlling the ego through discipline is a lot simpler than trying to satisfy it all the time. By gratifying the ego, one may get a fleeting respite from its craving and demands, but then it's on—on to the next gratification. The ego always wants more.

It's life on the mouse wheel, each trotting as fast as possible to stay in the same place. Endless effort, misspent on illusion. You can see why people are programmed into it—they are psychologically immature. It's all a bit sad.

"Trying to Be Someone" comes from an insecurity, which stems from the ego's need for observers and admirers. It needs acknowledgment and stimulation to feel solid. But leaning psychologically and emotionally out into the world—demanding to be noticed, trying to be cool, seeking approval and acceptance, trying to impress, seeking praise and respect—creates imbalance and weakness. It is, in fact, an affirmation that says, "I'm not okay. I need others to approve of me in order to feel secure." By leaning psychologically, you weaken yourself. Imagine constantly leaning forward at a severe angle, reaching out—you're perpetually poised, heading for a fall.

Trying to win people over and hoping the world will accept you for your wonderfulness is futile and weak. It destroys your real power; the stress of it can make you ill. Even if you get what you want, it rarely lasts. Today's success becomes tomorrow's rejection. Leaning psychologically is a fault; it undermines what you are. Gradually you become the manifestation of other people's reality—subject, of course, to all their fickle whims, moods, and power trips. By accommodating the ego in this way, you drift from the real spiritual you that dwells within—which is contained and solid—to a *fake* you that is brittle, self-indulgent, and powerless.

You can tell people how marvelous you are, and a hundred others can sing your praises and pump your worth, but all that is PR and hype. In the end, you're only worth the etheric feeling you exude. That is a spiritual, metaphysical reality; everything else is illusion and dysfunction. If you want to be accepted, accept yourself. If you want to be acknowledged, acknowledge yourself. Simple.

Let's leave hype and clatter, which are weak, and head to the less obvious—silence—where consolidation and real strength lie.

><><

CHAPTER THREE

The Silent Consolidation of Power

◆─────────────────────┐

Let's talk about psychological consolidation, then on to other practical ideas for solidity and calm.

My martial arts teacher says that when people go through the motion of walking, what they're doing, in effect, is going through a controlled fall. They lean forward with their upper bodies and throw out a leg just in time. That's why even a small crack in the pavement can tip them over.

Psychologically and emotionally, life is the same as walking for most people. They constantly lean into life, yearning, dreaming, pining. They're often dissatisfied with what they are and with what they have. Instead, they seek someone or something to lift them up. They want to be declared *special*—they want life easy, delivered on a plate.

In the process of leaning, they trash their emotional balance and drift from one gratification to another. They exist at the edge of their balance and their ability to control. One adverse condition—a casual remark, a small setback—and their energy collapses. Psychologically and emotionally, they fall on their noses.

The initial point in consolidating your silent power is to discipline yourself to stop leaning. When you're the most desperate to lean in on people, that's when you should exercise control. The game is called: "Stand Straight in Life." Not many have heard of it.

First, don't lean toward things you don't have. Affirm, visualize, and take action instead.

Second, try not to lean into the future by talking or thinking about it constantly. Instead, take time each day to make the "now" special, honoring what you do have and what you have achieved. Avoid what I call plan-itis. Endlessly making plans and talking about them—"one day, someday . . ." trashes your power and gets you nowhere—no results and no action.

Third, start to design your life so that you don't require things from others. Try to need only those things you can get yourself. And don't suck on people emotionally or intellectually.

When you lean psychologically or emotionally on people or toward them, it's a sure sign of insecurity. It makes others feel uncomfortable. They resent the weight you are laying on them, and they will react by denying you. They don't like your self-indulgence, and your insecurity reminds them of their own vulnerability; it rattles them. Animosity builds.

Consciously and subliminally, they sense the weakness your leaning creates. It robs them of energy and crowds them; they have to buy into your needs and emotions when they would prefer to concentrate on their own. They don't like the imposition, and often they react negatively, even if they don't say so.

Alternately, they accept the imposition of your weight, but then they feel they can take advantage of you emotionally, sexually, or financially. They will feel empowered to use you or deprecate you or discredit you in some way. Remember, when your energy touches others, they subliminally know if you're weak or strong—it affects how they see you.

I'm sure you know what I mean. Visualize someone who leans on you. Replay in your mind the emotions and the thoughts that their leaning generates in you. Remember how you react to their sometimes desperate needs. Notice how often they rob you of your energy, how in minutes you feel exhausted.

Don't do that to others; it disempowers you. A little unemotional leaning in some circumstances can be okay—others may feel pleasure in supporting you or assisting you. But too much leaning, and they will vote "no."

It does not mean that you can't ask for help—sometimes you can—but there's a difference between asking dispassionately for help and constantly leaning on others emotionally, demanding that they ameliorate your inadequacy or insecurity.

Thus, an important first step in silent power is *don't lean*. It's obvious, but most don't know it. When you're frantic for people, your needs have an air of desperation—they weaken you and push things away from you.

Have you ever had a romantic relationship where the other person was all over you like a hot rash, desperate for you? What did you do? For the first few days you probably enjoyed the attention, but on day three you gave this man or woman a hard time, and you started to tow him or her around by the nose. You enjoyed that for a bit, but in the end, this desperation and insecurity bugged you; eventually you tossed this person out.

When you're in love and you crave someone, if this individual keeps his or her distance or retreats from you, then your desire increases. If this person advances too far forward, your desire lessens, or may dissipate completely. When you're desperate for a deal and you lean into it, you push it away and/or you wind up paying more. It's called "wanting-it" tax. Before every deal, take a moment in the hallway to remind yourself that you don't need it. If you don't get it, it doesn't bother you. If you do get it, it will be under your terms, and you won't pay too much.

Even if your natural tendency is to lean into people—because, let's say, you're a very social person—*don't* lean. Make that a discipline. You can be social without leaning in. Put a sign on your refrigerator door: "When in doubt, lean out!"

Silent power often requires the contrary approach. When others lean, step back; when they cry out, remain silent; when they run, you walk. Stay in control and exude stability, even if you don't feel too sure of yourself just yet. Don't show your weakness. Be strong. Be brave. Internalize any disquietude, and work on it later. Initially, you may not be completely solid inwardly, but you can still come across as solid externally. The inward power comes as you act out and affirm your strength and control.

Through your solidity, you help others feel secure. They seek you out, life gets easier, and it feels much better. Become the sage, remain composed, be silent, stand straight etherically. Stay inside what you know— be content, don't have too many needs. Work on yourself.

Anyway, you're probably stronger than you think. Many of the people you meet may initially seem solid. But they soon expose themselves, and you can see that they are, in fact, in silent crisis—victims of their egos. Their real power is weak and polluted. It leaves them open and exposed to the ups and downs of life. They will constantly seek to etherically borrow energy, sucking on any life force they can find. They will have house plants that die and pets that get sick a lot.

There is a law in physics that allows subatomic particles to borrow energy for just a millisecond. The particle moves temporarily to a faster orbit, but an instant later it has to repay the borrowed energy; it falls (decays) to its ground state—a slower oscillation that it can more comfortably sustain.

Etherically, humans follow the same laws. You can borrow energy from another, but you can't inherit it perpetually. A small boost, and then back you go to where you were before.

Etheric suckers grab your power as you pass them. It depreciates you. At a deep, subconscious level, they drag you away from life and closer to death. However, before you get too indignant, I have to tell you that we all pull energy from others occasionally, especially when we're tired or emotionally drained. As your energy sinks, it's human to reach for the nearest life raft. In answer to your question, "How do I protect my energy?" I've included a few ideas in Chapter 9. Meanwhile, let's return to silent power for the moment.

People don't resonate silent power because, for most, the overriding issue in life is security. The ego's function is to keep you focused on staying alive—everyone is out and about trying to do just that. The issues of security dominate your psychology, everything you do, and much of what you say. It undermines your strength.

Everyone is silently preoccupied and worried about something, so the etheric energy is diffused and disconcerted, in some more so than in others. People worry about death and violence; they worry about *things* changing or dying, not just their bodies. Anything that has the potential to change worries them—the death of a relationship, the death of a job, the death of a daily rhythm that they're used to, the death of a privileged position, and so on. As I said in my book *Weight Loss for the Mind,* it's the death of things that scares people.

The mind functions in this way: "If this relationship falls apart, I'll fall apart, my job might go, and with it my lifestyle, and following that, my body may change from alive to not alive." At a deep subconscious level, an argument with the boyfriend becomes a threat— a life-and-death struggle—not just a discussion about the dispute in question. That's why people can get so upset about things that seem trivial. There's an energy war going on, each seeking to preserve their etheric life force while, consciously or subconsciously, they're in a titanic struggle with the demons of insecurity.

When they're not worrying about dropping dead, they're usually thinking about themselves, preening the ego with self-satisfying thoughts, brushing its little tail and generally making themselves as special as possible. If they aren't thinking about themselves, they're talking about themselves, keeping others amused with thrilling concepts of life in the slow lane. More often than not, they're calling on you to listen, to notice and acknowledge them, to observe them. It can be exhausting. Don't you do it to others.

Stay inside your power where you feel the most secure. And work on controlling the ego. Discipline it so that you move from its fragile world to the immortal certainty of spirit. There you will feel the eternity within you, and your insecurity will gradually melt. You'll accept life as you find it, rather than struggling against it, and you'll know that there's no death and no failure. So accept the comings and goings of life, and flow to your highest good with little resistance and great joy.

The more you control your emotions and the reactions of your personality, the more consolidated and powerful your etheric becomes. Once your etheric energy is no longer jerking back and forth, wobbling and squirming and falling over itself, a gracious solidity develops around you. Now you'll be able to see through your own etheric, to the world of pure energy beyond. A quantum leap takes place within, and a great perception descends upon you. But, remember, silent power is a strength you quietly express, not one you wield. It's born from the seeds of self-control.

The *Tao Te Ching* says:

> *To understand others is to have*
> *knowledge;*
> *To understand oneself is to be*
> *illuminated.*
> *To conquer others needs strength;*
> *To conquer oneself is harder still.*
> *To be content with what one has is*
> *to be rich . . .*[1]

⌖

---

[1] From *The Way and Its Power,* by Arthur Waley. George Allen & Unwin Ltd., London, 1934.

CHAPTER FOUR

Silent Talking

P art of learning not to lean is to get control of your dialogue. Most people talk too much, and what they do say is often just noise or irrelevant gibberish designed to keep themselves entertained. One of the keys to silent power is to control your need to talk. The rules of this consolidation are as follows.

Make it a discipline not to discuss your personal details with others. Develop mystery, silence, and a secrecy about your life. Don't allow people to know your deep, innermost self. Sure, you may have a friend you want to discuss things with from time to time. But, generally speaking, don't talk about yourself. If you have to, do so only in general terms and only when people ask you. Of course, sometimes the situation may require you to talk about yourself—for example, in an office situation where you have to describe your abilities. But, for the most part, keep quiet.

If you have to give instructions—or if you need to share your feelings when setting a personal boundary with another person, perhaps—choose your words carefully. A powerful person doesn't waste words, doesn't waffle and drift, but instead, thinks through what he or she wants to say and expresses these thoughts succinctly and purposely. The most powerful way to speak is with brevity.

Next, when engaging in dialogue with others, try to remain *underneath* them psychologically, rather than talking across them or even down to them from above. Let me explain. Talking above people is trying to make them feel inferior, pushing yourself onto them, or attempting to force your ideas upon them. It's dominating the conversation with endless tales of your experiences—hogging the stage.

If these people say they've been to China, and you respond by saying you've been there 19 times, you're trying to get above them, and you're being combative. Sages don't need to combat. They are eternal and infinite and a part of everything. In the "everything," there is no high or low, so they have no need to compete. They can just be. It's enough.

The *Tao* says, "Those who know do not speak; those who speak do not know." It goes on to say that once one has achieved self-control, "the mysterious leveling," a perception of the Infinite Self follows—whereupon life is not limited by your talking or by your need to define it, and you, in turn, are free of its definitions. Eternal.

The *Tao* talks of this process of self-control:

> ". . . *This is called the mysterious leveling.*
> *He who has achieved it cannot either*
> *be drawn into friendship or repelled,*
> *Cannot be benefited, cannot be harmed,*
> *Cannot be raised up or humbled,*
> *And for that reason is the highest of*
> *all creatures under heaven.*"[2]

This means that the sage is the highest because he or she makes him/herself the lowest—by controlling the ego (the mysterious leveling)—and disappearing into the Infinite Self instead.

---

[2] See Note 1.

Most people who talk out of ego, talk to hear themselves. They're not usually interested in what you have to say. While you talk, they're waiting to respond with something bigger and better. So, you mention you're taking a vacation, and they mention every vacation they've ever been on. Those people are dreary because they're insecure, and they have to win you over by trying to impress you.

Most of what people say doesn't impress you, does it? Mostly, it bores you. If the story of their vacation is particularly interesting or amusing, or there's something to learn from it, okay. But generally speaking, when they're telling you about their vacation, they're only pleasing themselves by trying to compete with you. You're going on a vacation, but they've been on bigger, better, more expensive ones. So, be careful with your dialogue, and try not to compete with other people. If they talk about their trip to France, and you lived in France for 20 years, don't mention it. Just listen to them. That way, you start to develop a style of dialogue that is underneath people. When your ego isn't leaning, pushing, shoving, and pressing upon them, you learn more about people, and you can love them and support them. By doing so, you exhibit solidity, and strength of character. It also allows others to feel supported by your presence, which grants you a silent charisma—silent power.

Silent talking involves first watching and listening. Next, it involves projecting love to the person you're listening to, or projecting understanding or compassion. You're getting people to voice their insecurities. You're standing tall for people by momentarily subjugating your ego's needs for theirs. Sounds weird, doesn't it? Standing tall and getting underneath others. But it's really a matter of controlling your dialogue so the other person can talk and feel more secure. You don't have to dominate, because you don't have to compete. And you don't have to feel more secure—you're perpetually secure.

So, don't talk gibberish. Most people invent things, exaggerate, or they don't know what they're talking about. They rarely have a command of what's being discussed, so they'll parrot something they've read in the paper, or they'll take something they saw on TV and regurgitate it for your benefit. Most have no access to real information, so a lot of their attitudes, and the information they do have, is secondhand. Stay inside what you know. If you're an expert on something, fine.

You can talk about it if people ask. But generally speaking, don't talk gibberish, and don't bother trying to impress people.

It's very difficult to impress people with words, isn't it? Even though you may have done some incredible things, the very fact that you're telling others will make them react negatively. They will compare themselves to you and either see themselves in a bad light—which may make them angry—or consider themselves better than you—so you haven't impressed them anyway. By talking to impress people, you set up a competition. It's irritating. It has certainly irritated you in the past when you've had to sit for half an hour listening to the story of someone's vacation in France.

You can imply power and knowledge by not saying much. At most, offer something such as: "Ah, yes. Certainly. I know. Uh-huh. I understand." You can exude silent strength with just a tilt of the head, by rubbing your chin, with a wry smile, or by looking people in the eye. Never forget, you're a genius until you open your mouth.

So, while others are talking, you'll watch and perceive. Notice if their eyes dilate, watch their hand movements, see if the color of their skin changes.

You'll notice if they swallow or blink, watch the slight changes in the muscles of the face, and notice how people shift position sometimes when they're uncomfortable. If you see their eyes shift quickly down on a diagonal, usually to the left, you'll know that's a moment of discomfort for them, that it may mean they're lying.

When you stand inside your silence, you're in touch with the feeling of the moment; you perceive and understand what is actually being said. Anyway, you can lead a conversation without saying very much, by asking simple questions. So, if you want a conversation to go a certain way, you pull it along by asking the questions that take it in the required direction. By asking questions, you're exhibiting an interest in other people, and you're supporting them. Then, if they come up with something particularly negative or express their insecurity, you can affirm positivity, you can affirm love, you can affirm life with just a few words. They might remark how terrible a situation is, and you can say, "It's not so bad. I'm sure it will resolve itself. Everything comes to pass, given time." You allow them to feel that you're there for them.

Be shrewd. Resist having to present yourself on the ego's stage. Quiet yourself and watch others. As you silently observe, touch them with your feelings. Ask yourself—silently, of course—how these people actually feel. What are they really saying? What do they want? Who are they? What is their strongest path? If asked, what is my best response?

If they ask you a question—whether you think they should go to France or take a mountaineering trek around the Rockies, for example, don't respond immediately with what you *think* might be best for them. Pause for a moment. Touch them with your feelings. Feel the response in *your* subtle feelings that is communicated to you from deep within their reality.

Everyone knows the answer to their own question, although sometimes they're not aware of it, for it lies hidden. At best, you can only tell them what they already know. Your "logical" answer will not necessarily be the correct one. By tapping in to their feelings, you'll be amazed how often you come up with an answer that is neither France nor the mountains, but something completely different. Something such as, "What I feel might be best for you is to stay at home for a month, completely clean out your house, organize your life, settle your bills, and get control of your affairs."

So, as you remain silent, what you're expressing is not only a humility, but a care and love for others. It's a finesse that comes from not having to lead. It's an expertise that comes from understanding that you're a spirit, not an ego.

Another part of silent talking I should mention is that once you're settled, you will learn to talk passively and equitably. Many people, feeling their disquiet and irritation with life, like to hurt others emotionally; or they're vindictive, judgmental or critical. They shout their abuses and try to deprecate people with verbal violence. It shows them for what they are: immature and chronically diseased. Don't use verbal violence to hurt people or to make them less. And don't be cynical.

The Cynics were an ancient Greek sect despised because of their arrogance and sarcastic contempt for sincerity and merit. They were nicknamed the dog-men (*cynic* comes from a Greek word for *dog*). The Cynics were known for their anger and their hatred of society, which they displayed by urinating publicly in the street—hence, the term *dog-men*. Don't be a dog-man that urinates on people's hopes and dreams.

Remember, anybody you criticize or judge personally has to be at the very same energy level as you. If they were not at the same level, you would either not be aware of them or, being in a higher oscillation, you wouldn't bother to comment. Always try to build people up, or at least be neutral. To deprecate others is not honorable, it's not necessary, it demonstrates your hidden anger, and it lowers your energy. By now, you should be past it.

Now, on to the more esoteric concept of silent talking. We all have the ability to silently communicate with each other. I don't just mean body language and facial signals; I mean communicating deep within. When people are talking to you, you can enter into a silent dialogue with their minds. Often what their subconscious minds tell you is not what their words are saying. There are several ways of conducting a silent dialogue. I'll give you a simple way, and one of the more sophisticated ways.

Of course, we're not used to the idea that we can access the mind of another, but once you know you can do it, it's easy. It's nothing more than just asking what you want to know. Look at the person's forehead, and extend your concentration inward toward his or her brain, to where the memory bank is. Your mind has to be blank. Then ask your question mentally, in simple terms. It's nothing more than a mental tap of the head—the answer comes back in your mind clear as day. It will always be expressed in the present tense—their subconscious self, the real self, has no concept of the future. If the question you pose is of an intellectual nature, the answer that comes back is short and grammatical. If the question you pose would elicit a response that is more of a feeling, or spatial in its nature, the answer will come back in baby talk.

Why? Because feelings and spatial information reside in the side of the brain opposite that of the intellect. As you know, in most people it's the right brain. The right brain has little dialogue because that is mostly the domain and expertise of the left brain. So right-brain responses are short, childlike, and usually ungrammatical: "I happy. I scare. I no like."

Try it—you will be amazed at how simple silent dialogue is. But don't use your ability to infringe on people. Just collect information, and move toward them or away from them based on their answers. Don't push them in one direction or another. At the very most, lead without leading by asking questions that allow them to find their own way.

The more sophisticated method of silent talking is this: Imagine yourself etherically stepping out of your body, and then turn to face yourself. Now your etheric body is facing the same direction as the person in front of you, the individual you're having a conversation with. Next, step back with your etheric and melt inside that person's body, keeping your concentration on his or her head, wherein the memory lies. Now, standing inside this person etherically and keeping your mind completely blank, ask him or her your silent question and exit with the answer.

Silent talking—there's more to it than I can mention in the scope of this little book, but if you ponder on it and practice, you will discover your own methods. Remember, we are all in a silent communication all of the time.

In concluding this particular discussion, let me ask you a question: When a thought goes off in your mind, whose thought is it? Most would respond, "Mine." But how do you know that a particular thought is generated by you? How can you say categorically that it didn't come from somewhere else?

Of course, people don't ask that kind of question. We're convinced that the thoughts we generate are ours because that's the way the intellect is programmed. It doesn't care for the idea of its domain being influenced by others. Furthermore, your intellect has no experience of other people's thoughts going off in your head. So it presumes that this doesn't happen. Not so.

My theoretically independent thoughts and your independent thoughts only *seem* separate from each other. It's an illusion of the intellect that comes from its limited perspective and its need to feel different and separate. In fact, there's no simple way of knowing which thoughts are genuinely yours and which are not. Other people's thoughts constantly permeate your reality, jumping into your mind unannounced, masquerading as yours. You know they do.

How often does this happen: You're at a meeting, but your mind is somewhere else—maybe you're thinking about going skiing. Then the person next to you, for no obvious reason, asks if you've ever been to Aspen, Colorado. These are simple mental jumps that we've all experienced. But deep within the subconscious, you're picking up all manner of thought-forms that drift in your direction. You're an antenna, and others are picking up *your* mental activity. The air is thick with a continuous flow of silent talking, flashing back and forth.

At a very deep level of consciousness, in the heart of the global mind, we're all connected. The global mind is just one molecule of consciousness, and it's in touch with every part of itself. I accepted this premise intellectually at first, but eventually I understood it, deep in my inner feelings. That is why I don't travel and teach so much anymore. I woke to the fact that I could do just as much from within the Great Quietness—and more effectively to boot. You can do the same.

Of course, people of an intellectual bent, experts in matters of mind, will tell you that silent talking is pure drivel. But they're quite wrong. They don't know because they haven't seen. Once you see, you'll know. The intellect is too disconnected from the etheric life force—the eternity in all things—and it's too focused on itself to comprehend the existence of dimension and phenomena outside its frame of reference.

I must say, when people tell me that these other worlds are phony and nonexistent, I always make a point of agreeing with them. It's a discipline of silent power not to argue. Arguing and debating is a disease of the ego—much like seriousness is a disease of the ego that comes from either arrogance or insecurity, usually both. I'm happy to leave the intellect alone. Attempting to win people over, proselytizing, trying to convince them through dialogue, is a thankless task. It's best to communicate inwardly and wait. Eventually they'll agree, or perhaps they won't. It doesn't matter. We have all of eternity to sort things out. The fact is, we are all inside the one collective human dream. That dream can be a nightmare or a celestial vision of exquisite beauty. "Yuh pays yer money, and yuh makes yer choice."

⋙●⋘

CHAPTER FIVE

The Wisdom of Non-Action

In the writings of the old Taoist teachers, there's a concept called *Wu Wei*, which is the notion of *non-action*. Initially, it's hard to understand. Wu Wei teaches that through non-action, the sage gains everything—that in quietude, meditation, and emotional serenity, the sage gains a knowledge of the God-force, of the eternal Tao. And in that eternity, he or she has everything, so there is no need to struggle or push to gain respect and material things.

In the modern environment, Taoist simplicity doesn't work so well. We usually have to maintain ourselves and pay the rent; we have to participate in modern experiences that were not available in 500 B.C. when the Tao was written. We have incarnated at this particular time to experience the wonders of the modern world. We need those experiences in order to grow. So non-action, in the modern context, needs to be slightly modified. We can take the *spirit* of the Taoist Wu Wei, however, and put that into our life as a further consolidation.

Wu Wei is effortless flow. The concept becomes obvious when we compare the difference between striving and working. Striving is leaning emotionally into a goal, a target—yearning for it, feeling pressured by your lack of it—tearing around like a chicken with its head cut off, trying to get it. That's striving.

Working is moving relentlessly toward your target, one step at a time, in an organized and disciplined way.

We can see Wu Wei, also, in the difference between effort and struggle. In *"Life Was Never Meant to Be a Struggle,"* I discuss the fact that many people consider struggle to be honorable. It's a bit silly, really. There is nothing at all honorable about struggling. Usually, if you're struggling, there's something wrong.

There's a big difference between struggle and effort. Struggle is action laced with negative emotion—struggling to finish the job, struggling to qualify, struggling to be accepted, struggling to win people over, struggling to make ends meet.

Effort is a natural part of human existence. You can't walk to the store without effort—you will burn calories getting there, buying your groceries, and coming home. Effort is natural.

Struggle, however, is effort laced with emotion. It is not the minimal action and flow of Wu Wei.

If you find yourself struggling, immediately look to see what the underlying emotion is. Generally, you'll find that you're struggling because the goal you're trying to achieve isn't coming fast enough. For example, you might have a certain financial commitment that requires money to show up quickly. Or you might be struggling because your actions are incorrect. Sometimes you're trying to win people over or convince them of something, and they don't want to be won over or convinced.

Sometimes struggle comes from having too many things to do—meaning that your life isn't organized. Or struggle can come from the frustration of having placed a goal into a particular time frame, only to find that life denies you.

As you learn to consolidate your silent power, you'll learn to embrace Wu Wei. It is really patience and flow—moving away from resistance and toward simplicity, relentlessly moving toward your goal with awareness, adjusting your actions as need be—moving without emotion and without exerting yourself too much.

Stay within your balance and capabilities, and trust the Universal Law (the Tao) to bring to you those things you need. Non-action is the ability to delegate, to be patient, to wait for things to unfold naturally. It's the ability to perceive where your strongest path lies. That isn't so difficult to do. Review your options in a meditation, and decide which way feels the strongest. Act on your feelings, not only on your intellect.

Wu Wei is manifest in the ability to turn back. Retreat can sometimes be the most powerful tool in your bag of tricks. It's the ability to walk away when things aren't right, the ability to leave a relationship if it doesn't work, the ability to say no when people are trying to suck you into actions that are degrading or when things don't fit into your ideas of spirituality, of proper action, of goodness.

"No Yell"

When you can say no, you're free. When you simply *must* have the job or you're obliged by need to act in a certain way, when you have to win somebody's friendship, when you have to have $5,000 by next Tuesday, you're not free. You're in prison.

So, Wu Wei is accepting life and not forcing it. It's being aware of the ebb and flow of the seasons, aware of the spirituality of all things, aware that in the great abundance of the God-Force, there is no time. It's knowing when to act, and not acting until you know. You can wait forever if you have to. You are eternal.

Wu Wei is being content with what you are, with who you are, and with what you have *now*. It's knowing that abundance, and experiences and relationships of real worth, come only when and if you're settled. When you're balanced, the universe provides; more will always be there. But Wu Wei is the act of not pushing, not forcing.

Be the silent, controlled person who's moving relentlessly toward freedom and away from restriction—toward your goals, one step at a time, in an organized, patient way.

Wu Wei is also the ability to get around the blocks you experience as you try to materialize ideas and goals.

When life doesn't want to dance to your tune, start by asking yourself these questions: Am I in the right place? Am I too early or too late? Am I going too fast? Do I need more patience? Do I need time to consolidate, to create an energy within myself that is compatible with my goal? Am I trying for something that's too far in the distance? Do I need to set a goal closer to where I am now?

Ask yourself: Is what I want appropriate? Does my plan infringe on other people? Does it require them to be something they don't want to be, to do things they don't want to do? If I'm involving other people, what's in it for them? (Maybe the resistance comes from the fact that you've forgotten to include them.) Have I looked after and honored everybody—made sure they are happy and ready to perform? Is what I want self-indulgent? Will it assist me in growing and becoming a better person, in achieving a more fulfilling life? Or am I just indulging myself?

Remember, many of the things you want are, in fact, dead weights—prisons you create for yourself. More often than not, material things weigh you down—because you have to look after them and worry about them.

Sometimes the deeper spiritual part of you, the infinite self within, protects you from disaster. You'll head off, trying to achieve something that the inner spiritual you, the deeper subconscious self, doesn't actually want. So it will make sure you arrive too late, or the person you seek will not be there, or the check bounces, and things generally don't work.

If things really aren't working, and they turn out to be a mess, you have to think, *Hey, is this because of something deep inside me—do I really want what I think I want? Am I committed to the idea or not? What are the consequences, obligations, and energies involved? Am I investing too much of myself in the idea? Perhaps it won't mean much to me when I get it.*

I'm sure you've had the experience of going for something and getting it, then realizing that the prize wasn't worth the energy you expended; it was a disappointment. So be careful that you don't hurtle off up some path just to prove what a hotshot you are, without thinking through your actions, whether they actually do anything for you.

The other question to ask yourself is: Are my actions powerful and appropriate? A few small, powerful actions are worth a hundred hours of diddling about.

133

There's a school of thought that says: When faced with an obstacle, whack your head against it until the thing breaks. Then move to the next obstacle, and whack it with whatever part of your skull still remains. I'm not keen on that idea; it seems to lack finesse.

When you're faced with an obstacle, step back and take a long, hard look at what it is telling you. More often than not, you can adapt and walk around it. Sometimes you have to wait while you raise your energy enough to flow over the obstacle effortlessly.

Don't whack your head against it. Stop. Get inside your power. Plot how you're going to get around it, how you're going to materialize the sales you need, for example, and how you can more effectively present your information to people.

No, don't use your head to power yourself forward, by whacking it on things. Instead, use it silently, to feel out where your strongest path lies. That is silent power.

From non-action, let's go to the silent, subtle nature of feelings.

><

CHAPTER SIX

Developing
Subtle Feelings

As I said in Chapter 1, we each emit a subtle etheric feeling. It has a precise identity, like a thumbprint, patterned in a complex web of energy. People perceive your consolidated power sublimi-nally, and they respond accordingly.

The subliminal feeling you exude is the *real* you. Life responds precisely and exactly to the subliminal feeling you emit. That's why sometimes your mind expects one thing, and life gives you something else.

There is a subtle metaphysical definition of *feeling* that is slightly different from the one you might be used to. If you tap the back of your hand with your knuckles, the impulse of that touch goes to the brain—and we call that "feeling." However, the impulse of that tap is really a *sensation,* not a feeling.

mind = "I think" - thoughts
body = "I sense" - sensation
STUART WILDE ◆
Emotions = reactions/responses

When tackling a problem, the intellect might say, "I feel we should do this or that." But the mind doesn't mean "I feel." What it means is "I think." Most of what the mind says it feels is not really feeling at all—it's opinion.

We refer to our emotions as feelings. But that's not a precise definition either. Our emotions are, in effect, *reactions,* which are generated by the positive or negative responses of the ego/personality. The personality establishes rules. When life complements those rules or ideas, the personality is happy (positive emotion). When the personality is contradicted by circumstances, it's unhappy (negative emotion). If your personality doesn't like you getting cold and wet, and you fall in the river, that generates an emotional response. Emotions are the reactions of the personality, presented on a grand stage and scripted in the theater of the mind. Free tickets at the front desk for all basket cases!

Emotions are the outcropping of opinions and preferences. If you had no opinions or preferences, life could not contradict you, and you could not experience negative emotion. Of course, the key to serenity is not necessarily in satisfying your ego's preferences. Rather, it's in *reducing* your preferences and absolutes.

Real feelings, secret feelings, originate in the etheric and develop as you control the mind. They reach through the quiet mind to the infinite knowing that resonates in the eternal coexistence of all things. There, you find the telltale imprint that each human mind leaves behind. In there is the metaphysical explanation for all human action.

The memory bank of this Greater Knowing records the history of our human emotions—individual and collective—at the deepest level of spiritual evolution. The total record of you is in there. People consider such intimate knowledge about others to be forbidden information. They find it scary, due to its seemingly magical and extrasensory nature. In fact, it's a natural part of our greater memory—our divine memory—to which you are connected via the God-force. You cannot be denied access to anything you wish to know, about anyone you care to observe. Providing, of course, that the information is contained in that greater memory, you can retrieve it. So, you can't discover a scientific formula that has never been invented, but you can see how people feel, at any one precise moment, even if they are at a distance. The process may seem occult and extrasensory, but, in fact, it's an *inner-sensory* perception. It's available to all, and comes from metaphysical sophistication, consolidation, quietude, and control.

The global memory, to which we all belong, resonates its own precise collective feeling, so we evolve inside a *group* feeling. Everything exudes the God-force, even inanimate objects. In addition, everything that comes into contact with human beings is imbued with the subtle imprint that our thoughts, emotions, and etheric mark upon the object.

Nothing much is lost, but sometimes it changes. If you play a CD, the music given off imprints on the walls of the room. Each sound wave is layered one upon the other. Eventually, we might be able to scrape off the sounds and replay conversations from hundreds of years ago. The mental/emotional imprint a human being makes in the greater memory of humanity is thousands of times easier to access than a sound wave on a wall. You can access anyone's imprint and know the most intimate details about him or her. By looking inside the infinite mind, you will know. But most can't see it—because they don't know the imprint is there, and because they're too obsessed with *self,* too cluttered.

Imagine a human with a 90-piece brass band playing on her head. The *"Oompah, Oompah"* is so loud that she can't concentrate on anything else; she's living in the center of a mental tornado. Her ego is strong, her personality dominant—all subtle feelings are swamped. The *personality* prefers to hear, see, and feel things that please it, or endorse it. The *mind* focuses on what is congruent with its desires, and eliminates everything else. Perception is thus narrowed by selection.

If you want to access the mysterious global memory and expand your silent power, here's what you need to do:

First, close down the chatter of the mind—with meditation, discipline, and mental control. Fasting is good; the mind goes quiet when you don't eat. You might also try a "talking fast" for 24 hours, during which you don't allow yourself to talk. Silence; time on your own; physical exercise; and a light, low-protein, low-volume diet all help in the general raising of your energy. Discipline gives you confidence, serenity, and power.

Next, start to exercise your perception by commanding your mind to notice everything, even the most inconsequential of details. It's part of the discipline of going from asleep to awake. Train your mind to reclaim the subtlety of perception that, over the years, you've programmed it to disregard. Our ancient, atavistic abilities were lost when life became too cozy and the intellect so dominant. Stake your claim to the subtle power.

Try this: Go to a shopping mall, find a bench, and sit. Make a mental note of every minute detail of your surroundings. By telling the mind that you want to notice and remember things, you force it to concentrate on life outside, rather than on itself. The "sixth sense" of inner knowing comes, initially, from a heightened sensitivity and sense of awareness of the *usual* five senses.

Watch everything at the mall. So if I were to ask you an hour later, "What color is the trash bin outside the ice-cream parlor?" you'd know—and you'd remember if it was full or empty. And you'd say to me, "Stu, I also remember the little tag on the bin that says, 'Acme Trash Bins of Minnesota,' and there was a Snickers wrapper stuck on the north side of the bin, held by pink gum three inches from the top—next to the scratch mark that says, 'work sucks.'"

"Good," I'd say, "and how many light fittings are there in that part of the mall?" And you'd respond, "17," because you'd counted them—and you'd remember that three bulbs were blown out.

Now, turn your attention to the passersby. Watch them carefully. Don't judge them, just observe. Before we get into how the people feel from an emotional, metaphysical stance, let's really notice how they look, and what that means.

How people look is often the same as how they feel. Over the years, your face changes to reflect your predominant emotions. So, scared people have scared eyes. Meanness shows up as an unusually thin upper lip and narrow eyes. Arrogance is in the upward tilt of the chin, and between the underside of the nose and the upper lip.

Anger is at the top of the nose. See if the bridge of the nose is pulled up—notice if the gap between the eyebrows is furrowed. Look, also, for restriction and pain in the lines around the side of the eyes. You'll also see anger in the shoulders. Angry people are curved around themselves as they try to protect their angry hearts—partly because they know subliminally that their negative emotions are likely to stop their hearts real soon, and partly to protect themselves from the pain they experience there.

Overt sexuality leans back in the upper body because the hips are tilted back. It can thus offer or show the pelvic area by thrusting it ever-so-slightly forward. When sexual look-at-me types walk, they must rotate over the top of each hip bone—first left, then right—to compensate for the forward-thrusting pelvis. The motion is ducklike and comical to watch. I know they mean no harm by it all, and watching the pelvic waddle of sexual seekers offers endless fun and entertainment—a real pantomime.

The other thing that will amuse you is the fact that humans don't think anyone is watching or noticing—obsessed as they are with themselves—and are therefore unaware. They don't imagine that you can see right through them. In the whirl of mental activity, the personality is blinded and imagines that nobody else can see either; it feels safe.

People make all sorts of tiny, surreptitious movements—movements that they are either unaware of, or that they believe are private to them. Their subconscious urges and needs, and the mental activity such urges create, show up in the muscles as minute body movements. It gives people away.

Your walk, your posture, and the expression and shape of your face provide an external blueprint of your inner self. People who are weak and insecure have a defensive upper-body posture, their eyes shift left and right, up and down, more rapidly and more often than a solid person. If you meet any true sages in the mall, you'll notice that their eyes move slowly, casting back and forth, or they will look straight ahead. Information situated to their immediate left and right will be picked up via their peripheral vision, which will have become powerful over the years.

To develop perception, you only have to ask yourself for information that you don't normally seek—visual and auditory information, and, of course, we can learn a lot by how people smell. We don't usually think of smelling others unless a person has terrible BO. But as you exercise that sense, you become more and more sensitive to odor, and you'll notice that each person's is quite distinct. It tells you things.

As you heighten your perception by watching, you learn very quickly—and now you're ready to heighten your subtle feelings.

Come, let's look at the extrasensory part of your silent power that dwells inside your nature-self.

><

CHAPTER SEVEN

Inside the Nature-Self

The *nature-self* is a term that describes your deep inner spiritual connection with the plant, mineral, and animal kingdom. Embracing this understanding is a part of the wider concept of silent power. Your body is made of stardust. You are alive because a star was born and died many billions of years ago; it gave you life. The iron in the hemoglobin in your blood traveled trillions upon trillions of miles through space to play a vital role in sustaining your metabolism. The iron in your blood is over 15 billion years old. In fact, you are a reincarnation of that dead star at a higher level of evolution. The rocks, the earth, the animals, all the creatures of the earth plane, are made of that same stardust. But we're not just interconnected because we are made of the same material; we're also interconnected spiritually.

I believe that inanimate objects, as well as animals, insects, and plants, all have a spiritual evolution. I believe that there's a collective spirit for the water rat, a collective spirit for the ant, a collective spirit for the eagle, and so on. Each species evolves and grows just as you evolve and grow. The nature-self describes your metaphysical interconnection to all things physical.

You're a part of a great evolutionary story. Even though you're human, you haven't completely left the lower evolutions of, say, animal; and you're not denied access to the higher realms of spirit, because a part of you is already there. In fact, you're spread across what may turn out to be countless dimensions that are hovering across eternity—growing, suspended in the greater understanding of the perpetual, omnipresent, infinite self.

The evolution of the animal kingdom is a pristine, humble evolution—one of pure spirit, uncluttered by ego. The animals have much to teach us in their ways. They remind us of a time when natural simplicity and flow reigned, before the modern era when the ego was crowned king of this physical dimension.

In the concept of silent power and your growth, it's vital to expand your awareness across these lesser dimensions. Silently draw upon the spirits of nature—calling upon them to heal you, to instruct you, to show you the simplicity and sacredness of their ways. You can stand by a tree and pull the energy of the tree through you to cleanse your body etherically. You can rest by a lake, and use the lake to heal your confusion, anguish, and disquietude. You can use the power of a thunderstorm when you wish to perceive a higher destiny for yourself; or the power of fire to cleanse your ideas and emotions, and transmute them to a higher place. And of course, there's the power of earth—sitting upon the earth and pulling up its heat, its energy from deep within its core.

The core of this planet, in its motion of spinning, acts like an electric motor. It gives off a vast amount of power. It's your power once you discover it.

As part of the greater understanding of the nature-self, there is also a responsibility that few people are aware of. It's the responsibility to project energy to those spiritual evolutions, such as the animals, that are oscillating more slowly than we are—let's say, vibrating in a less complicated way. So we love and honor the spirits of nature—the various species of trees, the things that crawl in the ground, the denizens of water, and the birds—to pull them up and help them grow.

Just as the dimensions above offer you healing, serenity, and freshness, so you can offer the animals a heightened evolution. When you concentrate on an animal, or touch it, it evolves. When you concentrate on the plants, the things in the water, and in the air, they grow. Just by loving a bird and watching it as it flies, its evolution is enhanced. So, through the nature-self, we create a spiritual bridge—a way out of the mental, emotional, physical existence—a way back to the lesser evolutions and a way forward to the greater evolutions above us. You construct an infinite bridge across dimensions of the divine self, through the silent self.

When you're part of the elements and part of the etheric, you're straddled across several evolutions—human and nonhuman. The beauty of the nature-self is aligned with the seasons, aligned with temperance and calm, with an eternal, infinite evolution. It is there, in the nature-self, that you experience the eternal Tao—the simplicity of all things. It is through nature that you pass and evolve at death, returning your stardust back to the earth once more.

So, in aligning to and honoring the nature-self, we understand the deep, spiritual evolution of water, earth, air, and fire—and, of course, the sacred etheric dimension. Bless the hierarchies of spirit and the group souls of the animals, and ask them to teach you. And in return, offer them love, and help them beyond where they are now—just as something or someone loved us humans eons ago and helped us evolve to where we are today.

Be gracious. Bless the lesser spirits and assist them. In this way, you empower your journey from ego to spirit, from clutter to clarity, from uncertainty to the consolidation of silent power. Be gracious.

><•><

CHAPTER EIGHT

Extrasensory Etheric Perception

To view the etheric, you need good peripheral perception. In the center of the eye are the cells known as the cones—they are used to perceive direct light and color. The cells at the side of the eye are known as the rods—they are color-blind but very much more sensitive than the cones. Over tens of thousands of years, we human beings have lost our peripheral perception, because we don't need it to keep us safe in the forest anymore.

The etheric is too faint and moves too fast for the cones to see. It's subtle. And because it's hard to see in bright sunlight and strong artificial light such as neon, the etheric is best seen in diffused light or the light of dusk.

You develop peripheral perception by engaging it—which is nothing more than telling yourself you want to reclaim that perception—and periodically focusing your attention on what is to your left and what is to your right. Place your hands to either side of your face, about 18 inches away; pull them back behind you, and watch them simultaneously, without moving your eyes to one side or the other. See how long it takes before they disappear. By activating your peripheral perception, you will, in time, see the etheric.

The other thing that helps is to have a more rarefied diet. It increases your sensitivity. So, if your diet is very light or vegetarian, you become more aware of the subtle energies of life. The other way to see the etheric is to fast. As you do so, your brain waves start to slow down, your metaphysical energy quickens; and as your metabolism slows, your mind goes quiet. Fasting takes you out of the ego's consciousness of survival, and you begin to straddle metaphysical dimensions.

The first of these is the etheric. Quieting your energy allows you to see out from within your own bubble of energy to the energies of others.

I have found that merely desiring to see the etheric doesn't work. To see it, you have to become an etheric being. Joining on an energy level, so to speak—existing in two worlds—moving your consciousness from ego to spirit, from finite to infinite.

In addition, I've noticed that believing in oneself and believing in these mysterious inner worlds helps a great deal in opening the etheric door for you. In the early days, I thought I believed, and then I hoped I believed, but some years later, I *knew* that I believed. That helped.

However, you don't have to learn to see the etheric in order to be aware of it, because you can *feel* it.

You can reach out and touch people. It's the act of moving your etheric or a part of it, with the force of your will. I know it to be true because when lying down in trance, you can, for example, direct your etheric legs to move downwards, and you will feel them drifting through the floor. It is not a sensation in the normal sense, as your physical legs are motionless. Your perception of the movement of your etheric legs is neither thinking nor emotional reaction—it's real feeling.

Back to the mall—sit on a bench where people go past, and get ready to touch their feelings etherically as they walk away. The reason you don't do it as they walk toward you is that you don't want to be unduly influenced by the way people look or how they are dressed.

The process is one of reaching *into* people. As a person passes you, visualize yourself with an elongated arm. Reach into the person through their center back, and grab a molecule of their feelings from the area of the heart. Keep your mind blank, have no preconceived opinion; just ask yourself: How do they feel? The first answer that jumps into your mind is the correct one.

Start by looking for evidence of simple emotions: anger, fear, confusion, boredom, happiness, and joy. Later, more complex mixtures come to you, and you'll start to discover intimate details as well as the more obvious stuff. Don't feel limited by a lack of perception. It doesn't matter if you're right or wrong. In the act of reaching out, you heighten your perception by demand. It's a numbers game. Try it on 500 people, and then on 10,000. Eventually you won't have to stretch to touch people—you'll know just by looking at them. It's an astonishing process. Through it you learn a great spiritual lesson; it makes you very humble. This human evolution evokes great awe.

Distant viewing: When people aren't present, it's a little more tricky, but it comes with time. The best results come when the person you're viewing is asleep, preferably in the penultimate 90-minute cycle of a night's sleep. The next-to-last sleep cycle is usually at a deep level of brain-wave speed, where people are closest to their spiritual self—their truthful self— uncluttered by intellect. If a person wakes normally at, say, 6:00 in the morning, your best time would be between 3:00 and 4:30.

Remember, this person is a thumbprint of feeling, so to find him (or her) you have to remember how he *feels,* not how he looks. It helps to focus in the right geographic direction, but it's not vital. Now, direct your attention onto the target and ensure that your mind is blank. Pull him back toward you rather than traveling to him or moving your consciousness toward him. In the inner worlds, everything is reversed—left to right and right to left—and there are some strange laws about backwards and frontwards. Mentally stand him up in front of you. How does he feel? What is his overall emotion? What's the answer to the question you want to know? Wait for his inner self to mentally answer you. It's open and truthful and will always respond. Get your answer and let the person go, wishing him love and well-being and good strength.

Distant viewing is a subtle art. It comes from silent power as you grow, as you know that you evolve inside a global molecule of feeling, which is infinite.

Silent power offers you access to many worlds. I can't go through them all in the scope of this little book, but I can give you a clue and leave you at the crossroads, so to speak. First the discipline, then the crossroads.

The discipline: See the world as energy, and become responsible for *your* energy. Realize that everything you do, say, and touch, everything you pass—even for a fleeting second—is affected and changed by you. You impact the animals and plants; the air, water, and buildings; and people—the energy of each drops or rises to reflect the subtle etheric pressure you place on it.

When you're angry, you impress that upon the house plants, and they start to die. When you're fearful, the dog sucks that up via its etheric and gets sick. When you're mean and vindictive, the energy of the room you're in starts to wobble and act chaotically. It metaphysically starts to implode. Anyone standing nearby will be robbed of energy and pulled down. Everything gets sucked into the vortex of your negative implosion. External reality shrinks and disappears—for you, anyway. That's why car wrecks are common when a person is in a rage. Their perception of external reality is lost—they're momentarily blind, they can't see oncoming cars, and reality whacks 'em broadside.

With perception comes responsibility. Understand that if you're infinite, you're everywhere, and you can be anywhere, and you are *inside* all things, and you affect them. Enough said.

The crossroads: Remember that the solidity of the world is an illusion created by the speed at which atoms oscillate. If they slowed down just a little, you'd be able to walk through walls. In an out-of-body experience, you have consciousness inside a subtle body that we believe weighs four grams. You can pass right through the wall.

In effect, physical reality is both opaque and ethereal—just a collective feeling. You are a feeling. It's only by habit that you consider yourself solid. In a sense, you're a collection of particles, but once out of the emotion of the world, you're no longer observable;

you're less solid. You transmute from being in the solid-particle state of physical existence to the more ethereal wave state. (See my book *Whispering Winds of Change* for an explanation of the metaphysics of particle-wave functions.)

In the wave state, you're an amorphous oscillation, existing at no particular place in space or time, with no particular human definition. That wave state contains your consciousness and can be driven by your force of will. So, through it you have an immense potential to exert yourself on the etheric reality of the global feeling. The wave can move, so you move. It's everywhere, so your mind can be everywhere. Silent talking takes you to all parts of the global feeling simultaneously. And it's simpler and cheaper than promos, hype, and the air travel needed to communicate with people's intellects.

><●><

CHAPTER NINE

Psychic Protection

A few words in passing on psychic and etheric protection. It's hard to mount a solid protection from the mental, emotional, and sexual projection of others. So much of the etheric world is beyond our ken, and we are all inside the same one molecule of the global mind and its collective emotion. We are all one-and-the-same human energy—in a metaphysical way, our destinies and our energies are intermixed.

However, when two people pass each other at close proximity, I've seen the etheric of one get pushed away by the other. So I came to these conclusions: If you're solid, well defined, and in emotional control—with a good sense of your Infinite Self—you have a confidence that brings a solidity to your energy, as distinct from the chaotic pattern that is normally projected. Your defense lies in consolidation and silent strength. And in being disciplined and well contained. Other etherics will not interfere with yours—they'll bounce off as you pass.

In addition, if you project love for humanity and have little resistance, incoming energy often passes right through you—it has no place to attach. Because of your spiritual perspective and the love you project, your oscillation is not congruent with the lower depreciating energy of the ego's world. For example, if you're celibate or you project no sexual energy, it's impossible for another to hold a sexual visualization of you for more than a fleeting moment. The thought-form slides away like a knife point pressed onto a slippery surface.

Your best defense is to have little criticism and judgment of others; and no rancor, hatred, or animosity. The best defense is to have nothing to defend. The more you're not locked into reality via criticism and definition, the more opaque you become. It's a type of invisibility. You're here and not here, in the evolution and distant from it. Trust in the Great Goodness to keep you safe. It will.

Finally, it should be part of your daily discipline to silently project love and peace to all whom you meet. As you pass people on the street, look them in the eye and silently say "love," and press that love into their hearts. Do that to everyone without fail, and gradually you'll develop a resounding sense of unconditional acceptance. That's the best protection.

CHAPTER TEN

Conclusion

I know it's hard to exude confidence if you don't feel completely solid. But you can fake it 'til you make it. Just by maintaining silence—not leaning, not pushing, not yearning—and controlling your emotional reactions, you dominate your psychology. You act out a silent strength even though you may not be resonating it deeply within as yet.

Don't give yourself away. Work quietly on your weaknesses, develop a reserve and mystery, be organized and self-sufficient, and keep your life to yourself. Knowledge is power. The knowledge you never speak of is silent power.

Consume less, stay in control, and be at one with your inner self and nature. Purify your life, constantly skimming, cleaning, throwing things out, simplifying. One morning you wake up and the power is all there. You won't have to cover up your disquietude—it will have melted away.

A great unfolding awaits you as you begin to understand that you can dominate this human evolution of yours, even from a humble position. You don't have to be a superstar. In fact, the superstars often show their weakness by having to stand out and preen themselves and strut, to mask their worries and insecurities. Most of the *"rah-rah"* is there to cover up an inner self that's none too solid.

Do this: Draw a line in the sand. Agree to step across to a new way of dealing with life. Set up a sacred week for yourself. Pray to your God, and call on your Infinite Self and the nature spirits and all the great powers to help you make the changes your need. Meditate each day, fast for a day or two during the week, and also pick 24 hours during which you'll maintain complete silence.

Read, bathe, rest, purify, walk in the forest at night, pull energy from the earth, become friends with water; let the spirits of the air blow away any confusion. Use the strength of fire to give you new hope and courage, and ask it to grant you a vision of the future. Let it show you how the God-force can warm your heart and how it will empower your detachment so you can consolidate your serenity and your poise.

And you—yes, you—you long-lost scallywag, it's time for you to come back to the sacred place to which you belong, and step inside the gentle embrace of the Great Goodness.

Remember, there was a time eons ago when our people had perception—before it was lost in clatter, insecurity, and self-delusion. Claim that perception as yours, and learn to touch the etheric, use the life force, and rekindle the old ways within you so that others might remember, also. Step now to an alternative evolution, beyond hesitancy and fear, beyond the common emotions; step now to that pristine place within. No matter if you can't see it yet. Believe and walk in. It will welcome you, I assure you, and it will teach you in the years to come.

There's much there for you to learn—strange aspects of this incredible journey that few really understand. Worlds inside worlds, opaque dimensions of spiritual evolution folded in on themselves, moving backwards in time. Creativity as yet unseen, hovering just beyond the intellect, waiting to be gathered up and expressed. Much wisdom and many things await, not the least of which is the great awe that pours forth from an eternal perception of self.

And, in your sacred week, pray for yourself and pray for all humanity and the animals and the little things, and ask that the Great Spirit descend upon us all. Ask it to help us restore a sacred, silent power. Ask it to open our eyes, so that over time the light flowing from the Great Goodness will establish a world of simplicity, bathed in the kindness of a settled heart—each human spirit gracious, respectful; and each contributing in his or her humble way to the greater understanding of this strange but glorious human experience.

The world of the ego will change in the coming decades, and, over a few hundred years, a new perception will rise from the burnt-out ashes of this evolutionary phase. People will want to return to the sacred ways of long ago—it will seem natural and proper. Eventually we'll see a world steeped in honor and balance, dressed in the unassuming vestments of unconditional love and serenity.

Embrace your silent power. Come. Be brave. A great awakening is yours for the asking. Then, offer your perception and silent power in service to others. Be subtle; don't force people. Teach by example. Lead them from behind, gradually, with a touch here and a word there. Lead them from their pain, out of the darkness, across the invisible bridge, to the land of perpetual light wherein dwells the enormity of the Great Goodness, waiting patiently for each to arrive. Come. Step. Your time is now.

❦

About the Author

Stuart Wilde has written 16 books on consciousness and awareness. His perceptive and quirky way of writing has won him a loyal readership over the years, and he has also had a lasting effect on the New Age movement. Over a period of 20 years, he has come to be known as "the teacher's teacher" because of the influence he's had on other writers and lecturers in the field. Website: **www.stuartwilde.com**

Notes

Notes

Notes

Notes

Notes

Notes

Hay House Titles of Related Interest

Books

After Life, by John Edward
Born Knowing, by John Holland
Empowerment, by John Randolph Price
The Lightworker's Way, by Doreen Virtue, Ph.D.
The Power of Intention, by Dr. Wayne W. Dyer
Sylvia Browne's Book of Angels, by Sylvia Browne
Trust Your Vibes, by Sonia Choquette

Card Decks

Archetype Cards (80-card deck and instruction booklet),
by Caroline Myss
Empowerment Cards (a 50-card deck), by Tavis Smiley
I Can Do It® Cards (a 60-card deck), by Louise L. Hay
Manifesting Good Luck Cards: Growth and Enlightenment
(a 50-card deck), by Deepak Chopra
Miracle Cards (a 50-card deck), by Marianne Williamson

⊰●⊱

All of the above are available at your
local bookstore, or may be ordered by visiting:
Hay House USA: **www.hayhouse.com**
Hay House Australia: **www.hayhouse.com.au**
Hay House UK: **www.hayhouse.co.uk**
Hay House South Africa: **orders@psdprom.co.za**

⊰●⊱

We hope you enjoyed this Hay House book.
If you would like to receive a free catalog featuring
additional Hay House books and products,
or if you would like information about the
Hay Foundation, please contact:

Hay House, Inc.
P.O. Box 5100
Carlsbad, CA 92018-5100

(760) 431-7695 or **(800) 654-5126**
(760) 431-6948 (fax) or **(800) 650-5115 (fax)**
www.hayhouse.com

⊰⊱

Published and distributed in Australia by:
Hay House Australia Pty. Ltd. • 18/36 Ralph St. • Alexandria
NSW 2015 • *Phone:* 612-9669-4299 • *Fax:* 612-9669-4144
www.hayhouse.com.au

Published and distributed in the United Kingdom by:
Hay House UK, Ltd. • Unit 62, Canalot Studios
222 Kensal Rd., London W10 5BN • *Phone:* 44-20-8962-1230
Fax: 44-020-8962-1239 • www.hayhouse.co.uk

Published and distributed in the Republic of South Africa by:
Hay House SA (Pty), Ltd., P.O. Box 990, Witkoppen 2068
Phone/Fax: 2711-7012233 • orders@psdprom.co.za

Distributed in Canada by: Raincoast
9050 Shaughnessy St., Vancouver, B.C. V6P 6E5
Phone: (604) 323-7100 • *Fax:* (604) 323-2600

⊰⊱

Sign up via the Hay House USA Website to receive the
Hay House online newsletter and stay informed about what's
going on with your favorite authors. You'll receive bimonthly
announcements about: Discounts and Offers, Special Events,
Product Highlights, Free Excerpts, Giveaways, and more!
www.hayhouse.com